Sky Mesa Journal

Sky Mesa Journal

Judith Deem Dupree

FOREWORD BY
Dean Nelson

RESOURCE *Publications* · Eugene, Oregon

SKY MESA JOURNAL

Resource Publications
An Imprint of Wipf and Stock Publishers
199 W. 8th Ave., Suite 3
Eugene, OR 97401

www.wipfandstock.com

PAPERBACK ISBN: 978-1-4982-8967-2
HARDCOVER ISBN: 978-1-4982-8969-6
EBOOK ISBN: 978-1-4982-8968-9

Manufactured in the U.S.A.

Ask for the Known,
and you will receive
the Unknown.

Ask for the Unknown,
and you will recall
the Known.

Foreword

IF YOU HAVE READ scripture or heard sermons in Christian churches, you have heard what the Kingdom of God is like.

It is like a lost coin, or a lost sheep. Or a lost son. A hidden treasure.

A traveler who provides help to someone of a different race. A mustard seed. A beggar and a rich man. A banquet. Workers in a vineyard. A person who prays privately while the hypocrite prays publicly.

A barren fig tree.

Yeast.

Those are some of the images Jesus used when describing the Kingdom of Heaven that is also visible, on occasion, on earth.

The images often refer to something of value that was lost, but then was found. Sometimes the images turned His followers' assumptions and stereotypes upside down. Sometimes the images left people scratching their heads, wondering what He meant.

Usually, when Jesus talked about the Kingdom of God, the subtext was, "You thought it was all over *here*, when it's really over *there*. You were taught *this*, but I'm teaching you *that*."

It's not that Jesus set out to confuse and confound, although that was often the result. He used these images to show us that whatever we think the Kingdom is, it's always more. There's always more to see, more to observe, more to celebrate.

Sky Mesa Journal helps us see that "more." The Kingdom can look like the rabbits blending in with the scrub. Or the birds providing and protecting. Or the donkey in its silence. Or the sky as a thunderhead takes form. Or the open land that reveals a mountain far in the distance. Or a creaky gate that could use some attention, but still does the job. Or the cat that messes up the papers on the kitchen table.

These are the observations Judith Dupree leads us into as we go with her on her retreat into the high desert. It is in the desert that, to paraphrase e e cummings, the ears of her ears and the eyes of her eyes come awake.

Part Kathleen Norris, part Wendell Berry, part Annie Dillard, this journal from the desert provides glimpses into what had previously been hidden, both in the desert, and in her heart.

Sky Mesa? Yeah. The Kingdom is like that.

Dean Nelson

Dr. Nelson is the Founder/Director of the Journalism Department and the Writer's Symposium by the Sea at Point Loma Nazarene University in San Diego, California. He is the author of over a dozen books, including *God Hides in Plain Sight*.

Acknowledgments

BECAUSE THIS JOURNAL *BEGAN* nearly a quarter-century ago, a range of significant people have initially or recently impacted my "exploration of the inexplicable." To many I owe a depth of thanks that is unarticulated here. For a particular few, I must "say their names aloud."

This book happened because Sara (Jorunn) Oftedal yearned to visit her family back in Norway. She opened up to me this great adventure, inviting me to "stand in for her" with her cat and clutter in a rough-hewn converted bunkhouse on an old ranch. Her reports of rural life had already stirred something primal and needy in me. How could I say "No"? So Sara is *primogenitor* here.

My first thanks stretch far back—the late '70's. An eager handful of wannabe scribes gathered around Dr. Sherwood E. Wirt, notable writer-editor, God rest him, to establish the *San Diego Christian Writers Guild*. They became Homeys from Day One. Several of my critique group, notably Glenda Palmer and Candace Walters, and our beloved mentor, first endorsed this evolving journal. The Guild, with Jennie and Bob Gillespie long at helm, has continued to affirm me through the decades.

These past dozen years I have thrived in a small circle of word-shapers, fine poets all—with only a few scraps of this shared. Carlene Hacker, Kathryn Robinson Huff, Meredith Kunsa, Sylvia Levenson—my life witness has ripened because of you.

Our village Writers' Guild offers friendship and insight, and honcho Susanne Barrett has graciously contributed her well-honed tech-ed skills, steady faith, and sacrificial time to help make this adventure possible.

Two remarkable colleagues of words and Word have undergirded and sustained me in ways unique. Brilliant editor David Kopp's unwavering friendship—and specific encouragement on this project—is nonpareil . . .

my personal turning point. Dr. Dean Nelson's life-impact, gracious support and God-infused *Foreword* is an incalculable gift.

Faith-brothers, Rev's. Dick Adams and Ken Kalina, have "fed the stream" with living testimony, prayer, and generous friendship.

Gifted comrades from my *Ad Lib Retreat-Workshop* days continually helped me shape life: Scott Souza, Richard Terrell, Pastor Derrel Emmerson, Joanne Irwin, Sue Cameron, et al. Our first speakers, Jim Schaap and Jean Janzen—still friends and role models.

The professional edit by Marian O'Meara of *FirstEditing.com* has been pivotal to completing this project. Her intuition, affirmation, and wise suggestions in the lengthy and difficult segment on the Power of God vs. the often futile works of humanity were a particular help and confirmation.

Last, and ultimately first—my endless thanks to Brianna VanDyke, Publisher/Editor of the beautiful *Ruminate Magazine*, who read the rough draft a few years ago and wouldn't leave me bound by my private instincts. It is she who has continuously made it happen. A wondrous stubbornness. It's called *sacrificial love*.

I bless each of these dear ones who stepped into my life and remained there.

The God who stirred up soil and soul to make this clay pot that I am, is too large, too unfathomable, too wondrously-intimately present to find words for. Like all scribes of faith, I can only try. I cast this handful of seed onto an unknown patch of Kingdom loam, praying for Rain.

Gratefully,

Judith Deem Dupree

Introduction

THE KINGDOM OF GOD? Huh?

Jesus kept telling us where he "lived," and that he would prepare us a place "there." Is our death the entry point? Are we meant to struggle on, doing what comes "natchurly," trying to be *Perfect*, waiting for an inchoate promise of an uncertain landing place too staggering to comprehend? At the point in life when natchurly undid me, I was given an enormous gift: a summer-full of half-weeks at an old, rather run-down ranch in San Diego County. I settled in as part-time house sitter. What I *found* there, at this huddle of aging structures and its remnants of ranching, was an unequivocal entry point to this Secret Garden of God.

It started out as a diary, a "keeping of the days." It became a chronicle of change. The flora and fauna of this arid land became a Holy Land, my writing a wistful monologue toward an unseen, indefinable Presence.

I was led on an inner journey by observing the antics of a broken-down donkey or a pompous Bantam rooster or birds soaring, by drawing water from an old stone pump-house, by measuring the earth's harsh horizon against what little I knew of Heaven.

Sky Mesa Journal is a day-*into*-day account of my unraveling and re-weaving. Light comes. The simple metaphors of nature lead me into a Land I always yearned for and never really found. The birds and beasts speak up around me. Not in *voice* . . . but in paradigm that places all things before him. They tell me more than I have ever really known of that *sacred understanding* which is his Kingdom. It happens down deep or not at all.

As I saw, I wrote; as I wrote, I understood . . . somewhat, somehow.

I find myself working through a long denial, a backlash of old personal issues unfolding. They shrivel in the sudden Light and leave me newly settled . . . and instinctively I turn outward to the life before me and beyond me. Here more pain is gathered up; I face an even greater grief. *Weltschmerz.* The disintegration of life on earth as sustainable, as renewable—*as sacred.*

My concerns gradually expand, or evolve, to questions we all address about life as we know it today. The world and its slow (and speeding) degradation—how does this relate to his Kingdom?

While I have found no definitive answers to ancient problems (How could there be, beyond himself?), an energy and new resolve moves upon that angst I have lived in. I *can* do more than draw back into my personal enclave and wait it out, beseeching him to come rescue his earth.

The pain of fully *seeing* pain, of *facing* evil is heightened. I am no longer anesthetized. I learn to weep with him. I yearn for things far beyond my physical seeing. I long for ways of reconciling with God . . . of reconciling humanity to God.

And now . . . . It is his Kingdom, I discovered, that is the summation of all our dreams and fairy tales, the answer to our fantasies, misadventures, inexplicable wanderings. It is a new foundation beneath me, a new perspective to take with me down the mountain. The hills *are* alive! So they *have* spoken!

Ultimately, this journal is about life lived on a larger scale for having seen the many small signposts raised before me. The small simplicities amplified . . . the mustard seeds. My whole life-focus shifted, here, from an indigenous plotting of my way from pillar to post (from church to cross?), to a growing revelation of God's sovereignty and my small-great place in it.

Because of this Journey, I have measured everything differently. Small things that often slid by me loom larg*ely*; mountains of my/others' making crumble before this new sizing. I have come to see "purity" as less a harsh trail to climb than a deliberate side-step into clearer cognizance.

The Kingdom comes, *oh, it does*, in the rhythms of ordinary days, in the pitfalls and pratfalls and the tragic and tempestuous...and especially, yes, *he* comes, laying It before us in our terrible neediness.

This journal simply tells how it happened, is still happening, for me. It has been many years since that summer. Nothing has ever, *ever* been the same.

ə ə ə

❧ 1 ❧

Like a quilt stitched willy-nilly

SKY MESA RANCH. A place I never heard of until weeks ago. This is to be my home-away-from-home for the next few months.

This morning—this Monday late in May—I unlocked the oversized and unwieldy gate, shoving it aside just enough to squeeze through. The old bunk house squats as stark and ugly as a boulder beside its arc of pepper trees. The remnants of a flower garden dot their dry bed, shriveled beyond identifying. Our southern California soil is already parched and struggling in its endless plight and April's scant bloom; the empty skies have won. Crisping geraniums sag against the fence. I paused to finger them, and looked back, down the long hill—perhaps like an ancient Israelite leaving Egypt, throat full of trepidation.

But when I circled around front, a long swath of porch drew me on, promising cool shadows, a great frame of branches, an eye-scape of orchard and hills beyond. I dropped my baggage and stepped up, out of the glare. A sturdy old rocker waited, wreathed in a shimmer of webs. I brushed aside the sticky film and sat on the edge of it, carefully—easing back gradually. Its oaken arms wrapped around me. The smell of land and all of its begetting was like a presence, a fullness in the air. I began to rock—slowly, steadily . . .

For the moment, it was enough.

❧ ❧ ❧

I am on an old ranch in San Diego County, not far from Mexico. One hundred thirty acres of gnarled oaks, scrub, manzanita, a sprinkling of evergreens in at least one pocket canyon, a few pepper trees. Wild flower, weed flower, and bush that would grace a city garden with their color, intricacy,

1

and spice. Two ponds shrinking in midsummer heat, the tracks of varied small animals dotting and smearing its periphery.

From this higher point of land among the hills that ripple from the shore line toward the mountains, a mosaic of life spreads out beneath and beyond—like a quilt stitched willy-nilly, with no thought in mind but to piece together whatever comes to hand. A *crazy-quilt*. How prophetic . . . .

I have come here to house-sit, part-time (half of each week for three months), for a friend who is visiting her ancestral home in Norway. Like me, she is drawing upon her roots after years in some lingering transition that defies naming. Her search and finding are very real, and have graced me with this quiet season. Thus an uncertain adventure has begun. Now I sink into my own season of search, which has, at this stage of life, less to do with geography than the soul's bedrock necessity. Since I cannot, for now at least, lean my heart against my beloved Colorado Rockies (my own heart-home), here there is time and place to rest and recover, and perhaps rediscover life.

The ranch house is worthy of *old* Mexico, dark and rough-hewn and spread out low against the soil. It is presided over patiently by Bea, a lively, wispy widow of indeterminate age. She has spunk and class and vision larger than her person. Assorted outbuildings of over fifty years vintage cluster around the house—several converted to exceedingly rustic cabins. Mine, once the bunkhouse, is the largest, with its well-shaded porch, old-plank walls, basic amenities, a wealth of atmosphere.

This land is alive with birds and beasts, seen and unseen. Their voices rise and fall to the times of day and dark. The domestic animals are ill-fenced, and it matters little. The four-footed and web-footed inhabitants wander much as they will; the two-footed ones of *my* genus are as laid-back as their furry/feathery friends. The Peaceable Kingdom indeed.

It feels so. How quickly so.

Life here is a throw-back in some ways. It harks of a simpler era—days I barely knew myself as a child. But I *do* remember, because it is embedded in all our genes, this place and pace that we have mostly lost. We yearn deeply for it. Perhaps I had forgotten such a yearning, beneath all the muffling competitions. There is soil in our veins, dust in our eyes. We are formed of it, formed *by* it.

The land was ours, we were the land's, to misquote a better poet than I.

But Sky Mesa Ranch is not *all* "yesterday." I have already made an interesting discovery about "today." Bea has lent considerable space here to her grandson for his small but vigorous foundation. Ecology is their focus—they have sent "feelers" and workers out in diverse spots upon this globe—saving sea turtles in Mexico and elsewhere, studying whales in Victoria and raptors in Mali, to name but a few projects. This is cutting-edge concern for mañana.

Another tenant teaches the developmentally disabled, coming home every day to unwind in the scent of sage. Past and present seem to weave naturally here—a mantle, a serape, that covers life better than any heated polemic can describe. Alas, it will not long be so! Tomorrow intrudes rapidly. I hear the bulldozers as I sit on this musty old porch. In the next few years most of Sky Mesa Ranch will become an upscale housing development. Only the original house and outbuildings will remain. Like an outpost . . .

I understand, of course. Bea can't keep it up, and she needs to assure her own future. I suddenly feel an inconsolable loss, however, as I'm sure she does. In a sense, Sky Mesa is *our* past and present, and future.

We are all losing too much, too quickly—even those fortunate families who have already settled into these cragged and crevassed hills, and hear the wild calls beyond them and see the displaced coyotes scurry in confusion across their back yards. Yes, they lose too, in the midst of their good fortune. Their stately homes are no match for the stark beauty I see before me. Beyond their windows they will see their own replications: home after lovely home—and further, oh, only footfalls away, barely beyond their rooftops, a few snatches and patches of tangled nature. That is a loss they cannot know, and we are all poorer for it.

Time does march on, to quote an execrable platitude. Time undoes our grip on those realities we held sacred, or at least *secure*—the soul's unsung necessities. Such realities of place and space were long our core, our heart. Perhaps it is our grief for such loss that scars us all, beneath our more personal griefs. I think that there is a well of tears within me. I feel my fingers slipping off this bit of rugged, harshly lovely earth. Perhaps I have come up here to say farewell.

And I have felt my fingers slipping off my own sense of being.

I think my grief is full enough. I have come here to say farewell to the past, to find a way into tomorrow.

ॐ ॐ ॐ

This was my first morning to wake up in this strange surrounding. The tiny bedroom closed in on me, filled with evidence of someone else's life. I felt unreal, almost spooked by ghosts of the unknown people who have inhabited these rough premises long years before I came.

Lying there, beneath an already bright window, I took a good while to think through the stories I have heard of this Sky Mesa Ranch—Bea's memories, and the hearsay of others who live here and nearby. Will my brief passage add a footnote? Of course not, as far as life and continuity on this land is concerned. As for the touch of this land on my life, I feel a stirring of fear and awe, and both are better than feeling nothing. I know *that* well.

I remember when I awoke each morning within a Light more clear than this sun, warmer than its enfolding. Morning has dawned too often cold and blank over these past several years, like a grayness creeping slowly up on me.

Really, why am I here? What do I want from this place, this time?

A sense of God, I guess. I remember that once I was *in love*. The Encounter which engulfed my small protestation of unbelief was a reality from which I drew each breath, as if I had just risen, Eve-like, from the soil. I remember the fragrance of that *knowing*—the incredible waft of pure joy that wrapped me, the sense of *Garden* all unfurled. I would have died for this great new Friend, flinging off the shrouds that wrapped my shriven, delighted, yearning self.

Oh, this was Grace! It was a gift that I hid within me when the torments of a thousand demons raged against my soul; it was a flagon that I carried into deserts.

I remember; and yet I must admit this now, and get it said: It is as if another *me* walked there, seeing, touching, listening. The deserts were so great, the storms so wild. I am so very human . . . Like pioneers who struggled over endless barren landscape, some shrugging off what they could no longer carry, I have left behind my tattered vestments of joy, the weighty evidences of love, the great, clear purity of passion that once brimmed my jug. The years lap in great, frozen waves across my lifescape. I see there the trail of discards of my journey, the broken promises, broken faith, my broken heart.

It was all so real; I can write about it yet. I can even frame it in passionate language, *as if it were still real.*

Indeed, why *am* I here?

I think that I am driven by a *memory* of passion, *a need for passion*, to sustain me. Not the cheap stuff, the brittle, the varied dark-tinged hungers that become so merciless, but something Spring-clean, wind-whipped, breath-gasping. I have lost my sense of *passionate*—the steady ripple through my soul of a life quality always and still unnamable. Not knowing *"It"* by name, its "unpronounceability" makes it no less real. *Passion* is close enough. I need it more than life, far more than hollowed certainty.

That I now know, for the loss of it. I am empty. There . . . I said it.

And so I guess I am *waiting* here. Wandering, wondering, feeling pretentious, foolish—as if I were a small charade of me perched awkwardly where Heaven or the heavens might encounter earth, if I wish hard enough. I am not sure what it means to wait; I've forgotten how. If I should sit here long, un*Visited*, and climb back into my car and wind back down the tortuous road, perhaps I would leave this season unfulfilled forever. But I *will* wait here, silent, feeling awkward. There is nothing left *to me* to do, nothing left *for me* to ask for except that *"It,"* a life-change somewhere beneath the silence that I bring.

For now, it is enough to be here, *simply be here.*

ཨ ཨ ཨ

Today I set out to explore the ranch. It is a luxury to do nothing, to simply tramp around, looking, poking and picking up and sniffing at it all. It took me the first hour to get used to the idea of wasting time.

Wasting time? Oh, what has happened to me?

I finally climbed a boulder and sat down long enough to wait for that lie to dissipate on the heated air. This *is* a luxury, yes, a necessary luxury! And so I have done little else today but look up and down and around and across, taking the measure of it all.

I am surrounded by rocks. They argue with the sky for space, filling each small emptiness before me, lunging into hills, rupturing into mountains. They slice the horizon into size that we can live beneath.

The rocks are a holy grain on his threshing floor.

The land out here *is* mostly up and down—but Sky Mesa is nonetheless a mesa, born of some geological belch or shift, one of many ancient "tables" that spread atop the Southern California topography. To think of it as flat, however, is fallacy. A mesa is flat if the surroundings are flat—as in areas of New Mexico. There, you can perhaps see in a straight line from one end to another across the desert haze. What surrounds your feet is pretty much paradigm of what you see on top.

Here, where the land is more a zigzag, smallish chasms gape and pucker, rutting their way up the strewn slopes, and hillocks lift their shoulders insistently, angular and unkempt as the lower footlands. They are only level from a distance. The mesas, and all their variables, were a surprise to me.

One could say Sky Mesa Ranch is a smallish noun, verbed out by the countryside around it. This corona, this jagged, rugged crown of soil and its scratch of horticulture, composite all the best and worst of our arid, lovely corner of creation.

And, in a way, all that lies upon this small uplift, all that transpires, that respires here, is a microcosm of the Life beyond life that draws our eyes upward. A parable, something of a parallel. The mundane, the spiritual, nature in its every aspect.

A table, a tableau . . .

I have to find the core of this thought; there's something here I need. I have an image of myself both looking back and peering ahead at the endless tumble of land around me, discouragement heavy in my knapsack.

Not a pretty picture. Like a tramp, a wanderer, I have dragged myself across the pocked plains and the gullies of my modest height, my "mesa," toting all my baggage, wishing for an *evenness* that will never be. What I have wanted, gut-wrenchingly ached for, these past few seasons (*oh!—for a lifetime*) is to reach some higher ground that I could walk without forever stumbling.

I am so sore; I ache bone-deep from tripping over life "in the trenches!" It never fully occurred to me that higher ground (whatever that means) might be no more level. Perhaps it only looks so from a distance.

I suspect, *aha!* that there is no level ground. But I want it so! I have dreamed it so, needed it to be so, felt the lovely certainty of *straight paths* beneath my clumsy feet as Promise. Oh, God!—if it were so, my heart would soar; my eyes would never leave you!

I would not trip . . . over my own missteps or the clumsy steps of others.

What nonsense I've indulged in! Why did I ever think that it could be? Hope has driven me, like a shimmer set before me; dread has riven me, dragged behind like a chain of broken pledges. Like a yoke I could not bear—and could not bear to lay down.

I have convinced myself that I must one day come into some great ease—that all my being will rest so lightly, so molded to his gait, his footprint, shin and thigh and thought that my knobby knees will never buckle and bruise again. Isn't that the Walk that we are called to?

Did Christ walk so . . . *so lifted up*, beyond the *downs*, before they lifted him that one last time? People were forever trying to trip him. Did his feet never hurt from stumbling? *He*, perfect Being? I didn't want to see him like that . . . not awkward, hurting like us mortals. He was, is, I sense, an idol I have placed upon a mantelpiece. Jesus without blisters.

Golgotha . . . ah, woman! Where have you been hiding?

I have weighed me in the heft of this moment's revelation, and oh, what a slightness I see! A mere puff of wind would dispatch me. And so I am smaller than I thought. I do not know whether it is more hope or angst that led me here for this, this *dissolution*—this time of dis-*illusion*! The ground may never level out beneath me! Oh, I am sure it never will. There must be rest here in accepting this.

I *will* accept this, as Truth enough. Perhaps I can begin to learn how to walk now.

"May your good Spirit lead me on level ground," said David. I suspect things level out only in the Kingdom—whatever that means. It seems somehow an invitation . . . a promise? I intend to find out. The phrase "phony faith" seems suddenly very real. Maybe it's the only really honest way to describe what's plaguing me.

I am sitting hunched upon this sun-warmed boulder at the highest point of the ranch, scribbling on a yellow tablet. My hands are scuffed. My head aches . . . *I feel like a pain in the neck*. It is hard to see much when you are all bent over. But there is a small oak grove ahead; beyond that, the path steeps down around the rocks and winds through the tangled chaparral to skirt a summer pond.

A jack rabbit leads the way. I think it is time to move on.

༖ ༖ ༖

Monday morning . . . my second "half-week" has begun. I coaxed my car up this corkscrew trail, struggled through the rusty iron gate, and entered a different metaphor. I have never been in such a place, never imagined myself in such a circumstance, certainly never day-dreamed for such as this!

This is not the stuff of fantasies.

I have seen fairly *little* of my world, by modern standards. A provincial, archetypical childhood and youth in Colorado, a short stint on Okinawa and in Hawaii (as a Navy wife); a few moves across the states, West Coast to East Coast to West. Adventures too quickly over in New England, Vancouver, Quebec. A week in Great Britain, and finally, a boat ride up the Danube into Eastern Europe. Visiting my relatives or teaching at writers' conferences, east and west. That's about it. I don't get travel brochures on my email!

My adventures have mostly taken place in a back yard in a suburb of San Diego where the eucalyptus leaves decay upon a blanket of struggling grass of varied "genres."

While I am not awash in a sea of teary deprivation, my nose twitches for the scent of faraway places. I have always had an inexplicable yearning for both respite *and* adventure, pursuing them with equal passion, perhaps simultaneously. Somehow they overlap in my inconsistent mind: a little nest on a hillside somewhere—and tucked in the nest, a backpack-suitcase and Eurail pass. My feet have itched to travel, and my heart has crept toward everything that begets beauty, tranquility. Both forever drawing, pulling, telling me of the schism within.

I *am* restless—always stretching beyond *where I am at,* reshaping the Oz of my imagined dreamlands—wanting to explore the next county or country or concept, to be saturated with adventure and beauty, discovery, understanding, while acknowledging, yes, the pain that goes with it all.

Strangeling that I am, along with this—a parallel, perhaps—a great incongruity: my looking back, forever looking backward into loss.

God has certainly known the deep longing within me for the "hills of home"—the mountains that were, for all my young years, a jagged etching across the horizon. *My horizon.* Their familiar dips and spikes have reared snowy summits within me at the oddest moments—a sudden overlay to congested city blocks or monotones of high desert, a contrapuntal to the drone and drumbeat of the traffic. A frosty breath of pine above the smog.

But now, now when I have finally given up my "running feet" (as one of my friends termed it)—and, I admit reluctantly, received the largeness of my own yard as a gift, this rather strange and dear thing has happened:

I am here! He has offered me *this* small and homely and raggedy and very significant gift, this home-away-from-home where I may spend these several days a week—*over a whole summer!* Just often enough to satisfy the real need for adventure and rest and a semblance of Rocky Mountains.

Yes! Here I am, propped up on the concrete-and-post porch of this rough-hewn 1940's cabin. What character it has—bugs, stray animals, furnishings that crowd the rooms, books and papers that spill over various surfaces! What fun! It looks a lot like the ranch outside Durango where I spent an idyllic week (in retrospect, at least) one childhood summer.

It looks a bit like the way I would live if my husband didn't come home to me at night . . .

It looks like a composite of my diverse dreams.

Ah, I am *here*, learning and leaning, and marveling at my good fortune! Surely this is a treasure in a clay pot. As I settle into the new rhythms of these old acres, I find my gnawing hungers beginning to diminish. The very gift of *place apart* is so remarkable as to temper, for now, at least, my contradictions. I'm almost embarrassed to admit it, but . . .

This smallish plot of Land is growing. E*xpanding.*

I can't explain it, really. It feels somehow as large as all Creation, as large as the Thought of God. And it is mine—simply and beautifully and exotically mine—beginning with the next step I take. I don't know where my feet are heading, but I'll follow them.

Here I come, Lord . . .

ॐ ॐ ॐ

❧ 2 ❧

All the thin-worn patterns

VESLA, THE RESIDENT CAT, was delighted to see me arrive this morning; she was waiting for me to unlock the door, emitting little "eeps" of anticipation. It has been for her a lonely weekend—with only a neighbor's daily essential care. Cats cannot live on chow alone.

Now she stretches out on the porch at my feet, her tail safely curled beyond the rocker. Cats need human contact once they have been imprinted by us. Oh, what a pale intimation and imitation of our need for each other—and for the Father who cools our fevers and warms our frigid hearts!

Vesla looks up serenely. Whatever she thinks of her new "roomie," her bliss at lying next to a warm body on a cool porch with an ever-changing critter-world to explore can only be matched by my present contentment.

Contentment? My thoughts don't sound like it! But with each discharge, I feel as though I am laying a weight aside. Catharsis has its timely purposes; apparently I have been "saving up" far too long. And so I am content to know it has begun.

I have confessed my restlessness. Now it shoves me into this admission: in my mostly self-induced tight places and deprivations and *imperceptions*, I have dwelt in both grand escape and great inertia—all at the same time. *I have been a creature of enormous stagnation!* Why? Probably because I have always been afraid of failure. I have to admit it; this is what I have most feared *within* me, where all the real stuff happens . . . or doesn't. *I have been afraid of life.* It has been easier to lose myself, over and over, than to face my lostness.

The ironies within us—how we battle for control! I became a people-junkie, a walking vortex who sucked up the pain and purposes of everyone around me. And at my core a "dream" has forever haunted me, consumed my few quiet spaces, left me with a dreadful paralysis.

One cannot cling to daydreams forever, or lose one's very being in the lives of others, but I tried very hard to do both. Surely this was discipleship, laying down one's life for others. The high road of Faith and Service—*the substance of things hoped for, the Way of the Cross.*

This morning I read today's entry in *My Utmost for His Highest*—that's what precipitated this catharsis. Wonderful saint of yesteryear Oswald Chambers aims right at me:

> *"The counterfeit of obedience is a state of mind in which you work up occasions to sacrifice yourself; ardor is mistaken for discernment. It is easier to sacrifice yourself than to fulfill your spiritual destiny, which is stated in Romans 12:1-2. It is a great deal better to fulfill the purpose of God in your life by discerning His will than to perform great acts of self-sacrifice. 'To obey is better than sacrifice.' Beware of harking back to what you were once when God wants you to be something you have never been."* (Used by kind permission of Oswald Chambers Publication Association.)

Ouch! Oh, friend Oswald, you know me so well! How we delude ourselves, how we wrap ourselves in Truths misapplied until they strangle us!

Truth misplaced becomes a distortion of Truth. A lie. That simple, that complex.

For some years before this ranch-time, I burnt my particular candle at both ends until the wick was ash, *until my life was ashes.* I became ill, more ill than I fully realized or others even suspected. I had learned to swallow my physical pain as well as its emotional counterpart.

I don't like to admit to all this. I'm basically a stoic, perhaps too adamantly so—but by the time I was fully caught in the downhill spin, I was more nearly a hypochondriac. My "stoicism" proved my final undoing, for I had never learned to ask for help until the time came when I could do no more—or less—than cry out helplessly . . . irrationally, yes, even inappropriately, as the frantic are so apt to do.

Why I am saying all this, in this way, I don't know. The simple facts are that I had too much stress and pollution and a genetic flaw, and caved in to the total. An autoimmune disease —that's a *diagnosis.* But illness alone could not have done this; the emotional poverty in my life was the crushing weight. Under all that heaviness was *a Truth*—my running away, forever running away.

A life of pathos? *It* wasn't pathetic, although I'm sure *I* was, for a time. And it isn't important to unravel it here, once again, to pick among the debris of a broken life—only to accept that it *was* my Death before death. It is sweeping the dream-dust from my soul, and settling the earth-dust firmly under my heels.

I made a pilgrimage of sorts to another state during that period—from a great need to tug at the root of whatever life held for me. I knew I had to anchor myself beneath this sickness, or it would consume me. I visited young, full-of-life people. At the near-end of the trip I flew to Denver and took a bus to my hometown. It had been a long time. A very long time.

On that small, sentimental journey, I looked at my old, familiar country through "unfamiliar" eyes. We chugged through towns I had visited or known as a girl. The child *I* remembered scarcely remembered them, but I saw in the distance the unforgettable dark rise and plunge of mountains, a jagged saw across the skyline.

His HighLand lay stretched before me there, large and vague and raw with winter chill; I knew that it was a promise—that there *was* life for me. It was at a distance, and I would learn to breach the foreland.

When I left there, I had not found *home*. I had come to and gone from a place and time irretrievable. *Home* was an enigma; I could not reach it then, or now. But somehow I felt soothed by knowing it. I was not a stranger, but I had roots that held.

I did not tarry.

Coming to the borderlands of his Kingdom has been a slow trek. There has been no pillar of Fire, and only a few oases to refresh me. I have made it across harsh terrain—across rivers, around mountains, up and down chasms, through a long desert. I have circled back upon myself, have dawdled in the doldrums far too long.

And now, I am here, where sun and shade are truly even. *And home is here, in this old-new acreage, for this small-great season.* This lingering is not misspent, oh, no! I'm not proud of my journey here, with all my side-trips. But, frailer and wiser and older, I am ready to see life differently. I am trying to see myself, and my neighbor, and yes, God, differently. Perhaps I would have, anyway. But I rather doubt it.

I believe something rather inexplicable is happening now; I think that I am coming upon a new HomeLand. I have to find the gate and stay within, stay inside some boundaries I have yet to see—and learn what it *means* to live here. This shaggy roof will become my covering, as God defines it. When I move out from under it, I believe it will be a sanctuary to return to in thought, and will remain so until he says otherwise.

I cannot adequately explain it, only accept it. It is enough, for now, to know.

I have to come back to this: I am the blindest of the blind, the dumbest of the dense. My heart is heavy with its broken dreams. But day after day, I will sort them, where they hide, and lay them to rest. Day after day, I will ask for his Vision—*the real Substance of things hoped for.* It is life given back to me.

I suspect this rickety, weed-sown soul-home is a very Large place, indeed.

᪵ ᪵ ᪵

Dawn crept up on me this morning, and I fought it. Having quickly grown used to the eccentricities of this small bed, it has become a cocoon of sorts. I want the luxury of curling up for hours, maybe *days*, with no intent past the luxury itself. But the call of a crow and the crow of a goose intrude; they are irresistible. I swung my legs over the side and contemplated the beginning of my day. I felt like a princess who slept with a pea, a boulder-sized pea, beneath me.

The mirror over the dresser flatly confirms what my joints have already accused: I'm no kid any more. It is imperceptible, the way the shoulders begin to stoop, the back to bend a bit, the knees to stiffen.

Life shoves against us in ways inexorable! Sometimes the jolt is earth-shattering, leaving us bereft of balance. But most of our infirmities sneak past the gate of youth, the barriers we have set with all our salves and salving promises.

We grow old, or not. The *not* is feared only slightly less in this youthfulness-driven society.

I am becoming rather shabby. For someone who once succumbed both care-lessly *and* carefully to the cult of youth, facing this "middle age" is more than the twinges in my hinges.

I have had to learn not to feel guilty!

Ah, but we have been told to Stay Young! We preach and teach the gospel of vitality as if it were woven like elastic into the very fiber of our jogging gear, imprinted with a bounce on the soles of our state-of-the-art joggers, pressed and shaped into an encapsulation that we swallow with our antioxidants.

I believe in health. Fitness. We are, most of us, a flabby culture, dumplings dropped into a lean stew. Learning to take my body seriously saved my life, I am convinced. But our focus is often amiss. Mine surely veered, I confess it, from renovation to a dogged and pointed self-re-creation. *In the image of vitality.*

When I was most ill, I was haunted as much by an *image* of aliveness as by the specter of death. It was a part of the illness, of course, a symptom of my failing perceptions as much as were the rashes and pain that crept over and through me.

I *worked* at the image-making. Perhaps it is the *fear* of unraveling as much as the fact of it that so disconcerts us. We have "seduced" each other so avidly into the pursuit of sleekness, of vitality! The fountain of youth awaits us at the health spa; aerobic has become phobic.

Ultimately I have had to come face to face with my*self*. I finally *saw* me—not only the once trim-to-thin creature who dragged her slightness around, but the broken image-of-God beneath. *The guilt beneath the gilt.* In the battle for health, I had removed from *victim* and become an aggressor.

Couch-potato-hood is not healthy. Neither is the narcissism which spends its life and substance on itself. I came close enough to that ego-trip to trip over it.

We walk a balance beam between life and death. Health is a way of toe-ing across, with a certain grace, without falling heavily on either side.

With his rod and his staff he will steady me.

ào ào ào

A great fist of a cloud rose up before me as I drove east this morning. It threatened like a bully, full of braggadocio. I have seen such knuckled skies before. Gathering their small or large ferocities together, they spit and grumble, full of empty darkness. Much like a young boy practicing his *macho.*

Rain comes to us more often from a heaviness that rolls in, unfolding a seamless gray quilt of clouds, rumpled, bunched, tufted lightly. So I can relish the show of this pretentious blusterer—knowing, alas, that its threats hold no promise.

But, what a beauty! For some reason I am reminded of Shakespeare's villains, all painted larger than life. We can only squirm in our seats with dread anticipation, beneath the klieg lights, when Iago stalks the stage like a lean old lion, full of craft and hunger unassuaged.

Brrr . . . the quality of mercy betrayed with wicked splendor!

A cloud is a cloud. Maybe. But such a force as this consumes the sky with presence. It is presumptuous with the *semblance* of power, too intense, too dramatic to ignore its fierce metastasizing. It consumes the air, the eye, the very light behind it.

There have been such people in my life, and I have "worshiped" the semblance within them. I have cowered before their thunder, untouched though I was by real danger. They drove me under cover, where I hunched against their postulations and dismissed my own feeble *"Yes, but's"* as irrelevant or somehow unkind . . . as if the universe spun on the thread of their position. Ah, the unkindness was of another sort!

I have yet to "sort it out," and here I must. I am not yet real in the ways that count; this is my own neurotic response. I think it was once more my sense of "fitness"—a striving for proper proportion, perhaps a distaste for *seeming* emotionally unseemly—that checked me, rendered me mum, far more than any intrinsic equanimity.

I sense this response now as *in part* a failure, a lie, an excess on the opposite end of the scale of equanimity. The "honey" of gratitude cannot mask the taste of despair. It is essential that I find a better balance—a way to be real and vulnerable *and* invulnerable—with those around me. Without drama, and certainly without the trap of self-pity that finally caught me in its vise.

Yes, power has always frightened me, I suspect. Whatever within a person drives them to their thunderous or tightly-held necessities causes them to loom before, above, us "placid" sorts—us placators. I have trembled for a lifetime when faced with the storms that rage within the human soul. I am Dorothy in my pretty red shoes, toes curled hard against the soles.

There has been darkness in my life too deep to walk through. I have scratched out tunnels and crawled through with bleeding hands, in rock-hard places. For most of those years, I dug through in near solitude, slugging it out uneasily with my own clouded nature.

And yet, I still cower before displays of trauma and drama—bow uneasily, within, before such people, as if the semblance were a prophecy fulfilled, an ordination. Perhaps because the image itself conveys such *authority*. One who has established himself/herself as somehow inviolate, as unassailable, as burdened with imperatives . . . ah, such grand presumption!

Perhaps because I am so acutely aware of my fumbling, my own fragility, I stand in awe before one who ascends in a cloud of bluster. I cannot contend with life thus, nor with life's contenders.

Am I jealous? Maybe, a little; maybe more *dismayed*. But I cannot dispel such cumulonimbus with my small huff and puff. My protests fall like dead leaves caught in a downdraft. I am left breathless, speechless.

The scripture speaks of words arrayed futilely against the Word. I sense that within the impetus of God there is a catching up, an updraft that comes suddenly, like a great swoop of air across a prairie. Such Wind knows the darkening bluff of a cloud.

Jesus said *"The wind blows where it wills. You hear its sound, but you cannot tell where it comes from or where it is going."* It goes where it must.

True power is not fragile, but it comes lightly, carrying more than its own weight, heavy-laden with overtones of strength beyond its small capacity.

God told Elijah to go stand on the mountain, where he would pass by.

> *"Then a great and powerful wind tore the mountains apart and shattered the rocks before the Lord, but the Lord was not in the wind. After the wind there was an earthquake, but the Lord was not in the earthquake. After the earthquake came a fire, but the Lord was not in the fire. And after the fire came a gentle whisper . . ."*

Oh, let me hear that whisper—to drown out the thunder in my ears!

The wind has struck again—the hot summer *Santa Ana* that Southern California knows too well. Dust from the eucalyptus leaves sifts in the late afternoon light, filters through ragged screens into the dim interior of the living room.

Dust everywhere! Thus I am cleaning house—a somewhat haphazard process. My absentee-tenant friend and I share many strengths and weaknesses, including our rather absentmindedness toward housework. I have, though, always pretended a not-so-secret conviction that the principle of *chosen* disorder is as much a strength as a weakness. Not so, and I know it; my rationalizations generally fail me! Bringing order out of chaos *is* creativity, *is* genesis.

The kitchen floor was becoming "ripe" with my detritus. It was either *wash* it or sprout seeds on it. Now the light crust upon the floor, which served it as disguise, as camouflage, as much as a deterrent to blessed bare-footedness, is gone. The truth of its linoleum, its ugly gray swirls, is mitigated by the new, present purity.

Smug and satisfied, I drop a corn chip regally upon it, pick it up, pop it into my mouth. *"You could eat off my floor,"* I say to the kitty, *"for the moment."* Vesla seems uncertain, high-footing it gingerly as if she stepped over unseen hurdles. The house will not be this clean again until the day I leave.

Crusts do build up. More times than I care to admit, I have carefully stepped around "minor blotches" newly laid upon tile. Upon life.

I am not unlike this foot-worn, age-defeated flooring. When I submit to such a gritty scraping of my crusted habits, I wonder if I will breathe more freely somewhere within, where gifting lies? Grime upon ugliness . . . my "crusts" are an ugliness that hides my *sense* of ugliness! I don't think I've ever quite "seen" this before. The build-ups that inhabit and "habit" me I seldom fully perceive. I think them part of me in some intrinsic way—as, perhaps, a blur upon my pour of genes, set and settled to a shape and pattern once Designed.

Seeing the accumulation, the ugliness that both hides and aggravates what I have hidden and despaired of—my rawness, my unsettledness—is a woe I too often avoid.

All the thin-worn patterns of myself, my ways of shuffling back and forth through life, the spills and subterfuges . . . ah, they have left their tracks and traces irrevocably; there's no denying them, no magic cure that could belie such ruts.

Only Grace suffices.

My physical "veneer" is much more intricately laid than this. My face no longer supports the delicate artifice of camouflage; tints and hues cling there like dust blown over me, like smudges that have settled down on cracks too worn to cover.

The body is decaying; the bloom beneath the tinted bloom has faded, as every poet has lamented! But this is *my* encrusted visage in the mirror, stripped to its erosions! This is *my* tracked and cracked and blurry face! The image seen smiles back at me, full of sudden, ageless wit, and ripe with foolishness and wonder. Its lines are embedded deeper with the shuffling years, but I have earned this face, with its *youngering me* beneath the older me—learned to like it well enough to begin to greet it back each day, accepting it.

This is me; this is *my* soul, this ungainly, often still-adolescent *being* down under all the years of patterning. Perhaps . . . oh no, certainly, what I see is, overtly, less—far less than what I get—and more than I have ever deserved.

❧ ❧ ❧

When I returned from my nature hike, just before a radiant sunset last night, I was taken with delight by the cactus apples (or pears, variously called) that were ripening along the fence. What a splendid spread! They bordered each broad slab of leaf—*ear*, they call it—of each stand of pale blue-green succulent. About the size and shape of a porcupine's tail, the ears glowed with their great red-golden jewels in the evening light. I edged up close and examined them; their skin was smooth and unmottled, except for small, dark spots that looked like those of a pineapple.

They were too pretty to pass up, so I reached for one and gave it a twist. Oh, but a handful of miniature needles punctured my poor flesh! What I could not see in the rosy glow of evening was the nature of those small, dark spots on the fruit! Each held myriad infinitesimal darts—which were dug into my palm and fingers. This city girl was betrayed by her ignorance!

It was a *longggg* evening! To locate each tiny stalk, I used a magnifying mirror—set at a particular angle to catch reflected light. Getting a grip on it was problematic; the tweezers were cheap and crude. It was rather like uprooting a crocus with a steam shovel. After more trials and errors than I care to admit, I realized that only one side of the tip on the tweezers "tweezed" finely enough to grasp such a fine thread of rue—*occasionally,* even if I succeeded in coming at it at the right angle and centered it properly.

Finally, I could begin to see where the remaining darts were hiding (whatever is unseen is hidden, right?) by the small, pink, feverish spots that appeared on my epidermis. Aha—now the battle was more even. My body was fighting back!

I wonder how much this fruit resembled the Original Fruit? The varied implications here are too blatant to bother describing. What we see is not always what we get; like Eve, I got more than I bargained for. While this little indiscretion will hardly haunt the human race, the metaphor was not wasted on me. I pray that when I reach for anything, *anything*, I will check it thoroughly in Light more clear and less rosy with illusion.

One dart remains, broken off at skin-level—right where my pencil rests on the side of my finger. As if, perchance, I need a reminder.

A thorn in the flesh . . .

My early brother, Paul—ah, I know he knew!

ə♭ ə♭ ə♭

Late morning. Kitty and I sit on the porch together—I in the old rocker, feet propped on a rough-plank stool. Vesla uses it for a scratching post during confinement, which is obviously quite acceptable with her mistress, from the look of it. I think everyone should make such a stool, both for cats and *feets.*

Kitty has settled beside me on the equally rough-hewn table which is draped with a faded, checked cloth, dusty and dotted with detritus. Vesla has accepted me as friend on new terms. At first, in her anxiety over "mama" leaving and the uncertainty of my coming, she belabored rather badly. She was incessant in her bids for attention. I did the best I could until I would finally scoop her up and deposit her on the other side of the room. She ultimately understood.

Now I have begun to discipline her, albeit gently. To train her—to restrain her clamoring for constant lap privileges. Consistently and firmly, I set her to my side, keeping my hand on her lightly to resist her clamoring, stroking her lightly, rubbing her back, scratching her chin. Over and over we have played this game. When I am writing and she insists on my lap, I remove her to the floor, and we start over. She is fairly convinced, and fairly content. Her "wants" are more equable; we may be companions now.

He has been teaching me, like Vesla, that love is a gift to receive, never to insist upon.

Those of us who are intrinsic nurturers are particularly in danger of "burnout," of falling into the same pit from which we rescue others. Ah, yes . . .

I remember too well the worst several years. It was hard for those around me to face this huge, yawning chasm within me. Like Vesla, I crept up too close, too often, to those few I perceived as supporters, as comforters. I could see the dismay and hear the evasions—and several distorted fragments of judgment which passed from mouth to mouth and, ultimately, back to me.

We all have different reasons for our terrible greed for attention and affection, but the reasons seem to narrow down to the same basic fears. Whatever the driving pain, it is an insatiable hunger for others' understanding and validation. *Acceptance, right now, in the midst of our unloveliness, our unlovableness.*

It is like saying *"I cannot love me; please say that you can!"*

Oh, how we fear this unlovedness! How we fear each other! How loathe we are to face those awful needs in each other! It is not a pleasant thing—no, not pleasant at all, to be plucked at by another who is so unwhole. And, yes, the fierce needs we see in others are frightening and frightful, more so because of our own neediness and the blindness of it. We see their imbalance generally more clearly than our own. We are put off by such a leeching and leaching; we cannot sustain our sustaining of these lost souls, lest we be engulfed. We walk away.

But it is not only the *us* of us that others need, after all. Our best is too slight a gift for the restoration of a human soul. It is us and more that fills all the chasms of grief and loneliness and angst too deep to name—the need and greed for Love that "will not let us go."

In the Kingdom there is Someone to turn to, to talk to, to lean our unsupportable weight of soul upon. There is One who never wearies of our importuning. He never turns us away, turns his back, looks over our shoulder impatiently, regards us blandly, draws a shade down between us, discusses our frailties behind our backs. We do all this, and more, fairly often. We are judges and judged, each of us.

Vesla—"Little One" in Norwegian. With her head propped casually on my knee, the rest of her sprawls alongside me, a picture of contentment—no longer demanding or anxious or fearful of leaving her sanctuary. Kitty is at peace and soaks up my affection without demanding more. You see, in the midst of my frustration, I remembered this:

I will never, ever forget how it feels to be alone in the universe, in the midst of "living."

I knew how Vesla felt. Her world was all askew. Patience and a measured, measureless focus—this is the gift he gives us in each other, for each other . . . when we are willing to be vulnerable to him. There are ways of loving without strangling, ways of affirming, accepting without risking our own soul's violation. We do not know them, cannot offer them, until we have felt the firm stroke of our Father's hand.

Those few who endured with me, and asked—really asked—and listened, really listened, and loved, *really* loved . . . and stayed . . . ah, but they are Gifts of Life to me. They gave me back my life! The others were, like me, rife with their own pain and perplexities and purposes. God bless us all.

In the Kingdom, we are enfolded against a heartbeat that is greater than words, and sent to each other sensitized to greater pain than we wish to hear of. But readied. Endowed with a flawless answer shaped to the dimensions of our own being—Christ . . . Christ, and our firm and gentle hand.

Miguel de Unamuno said it thus: *"The solitudes of the soul You fill, and make of solitary men a man. You unite us. . . ."* Because he has been there.

When I, "Vesla—Little One," curl up next to him, beside one of his willing witnesses, it is the very act of acceptance that heals. Wisdom comes, healing comes, simply from our shared response, from the lovely balm of someone's patience, from the well of their unfettered concern. There is no greater gift.

❧ 3 ❧

For more than a fragment of time

ANOTHER WEEK BEGINS, AND I have returned to my abiding place, separated myself from my familiar and busy rounds these several days. I marvel at the disparity between the two lives I now lead! It is a type of co-existence that I could only speculate on, sensing vaguely my need for something akin to this.

I am grateful and humbled at such largesse and beauty before me—and surprised, amused, and a bit rueful to acknowledge that I almost have to force myself to come back each week. Once here, I wonder at my reluctance.

I *think* I understand: we are all of us so caught up in our smallish cycles of living within this great cycle of being. I am a "product" or victim (and willing instigator!) of this emotional spinning. It is normal enough. It is also limiting; we become too entranced or compelled—constrained by the facts and acts of living—to dare or choose to create a larger pattern from the cloth of our days.

I could not have done this, this uprooting years ago, when I needed it so badly. I was awkwardly releasing my no-longer children *and* mothering my parents. But what I could, *should* have done, I didn't do—find ways of attending to that part of me which needed Sabbath. Even my play-time and pray-time were consumed by the make-shift. People became my soul's necessity. I rummaged and fed at springs and larders no more filled than my own. We do that.

Now I am paced by other exigencies than those that bound me; there are always urgencies that replace the ones past. And there is always a yearning that only people can fill. It is a good thing to stoke on friendship and probe gently for sustenance, and to open one's cupboards, literally and figuratively, to those who need *what one has*.

But in certain ways, we may go too far beyond that. I did. We scrape off each other's surfaces looking for something vital, eternal, and too often we fail—both in the finding and the offering. We cannot give nor find what isn't there in sufficient measure to measure. *We rob.*

He said, *"Seek ye first the Kingdom of God and His righteousness, and all else shall be added unto you."*

I don't think we really believe that seeking his quiet shelter is the way to cultivate friends and/or solve our problems. We don't *act* as if we believe that. I see too many haunted faces. I was one of them once, and have stepped across that line more than a few times since.

My life has cycled yet again; now I admit to what I most require, even as I admit to fighting it. Now it is *time* that is today's requirement—my daily bread. I hate writing only slightly less than *not* writing. I avoid Silence only half a measure less than I long for it. And I set aside these three days for the pilgrimage to Sky Mesa, looking back at my urban nest like Lot's wife, like the Israelites mourning their lost Egyptian comforts.

Here, I am face to face with *me*. It is daunting. No rationalizations work here. The Kingdom has been held fast, and I am privileged to unlock the rusty gate, push aside the sagging screen door, and fit my key into the lock.

The key to the Kingdom. There's no sneaking in under the gate.

"Blessed are they who hunger and thirst for righteousness, for they shall be filled."

It is a terrible hunger which brings me here.

❧ ❧ ❧

Vesla joins me on the porch now; it is growing cool, with hints of sunset in the late day shadows. Cats prowl at this time of day. I have watched them uncurl and rise, stretch so felinely, shake off their inertia and stand poised, nose to the wind, waiting. Probably little bugs and beasties come out to feed now. Lizards scuttle across the warm, hard clay, seeking out their smaller delicacies. The unending chain of life.

Vesla is well-fed. But her tongue says, "Hmm, lizard chops! Fie upon Kitty Krispies!" I understand. In my spiritual inertia, I have often settled for Gospel Glitter or Scripture Scramble when what I taste within me is some unnamed, even unnamable *Presence*. My soul is starved.

I have weighed me in the heft of this moment's revelation, and oh, what a slightness I see! A mere puff of wind would dispatch me.

And so I am smaller than I thought.

We want to be "larger than life," whatever that means to us. We want to hold *life* close to our *great* hearts and carry it reverently, nurture it, honoring the Gifter.

And then we drop it all; our wobbly arms fall, like Moses' were apt to. It all dribbles from our awkward clutch.

Our *clutch* . . . .

Life is too large to gather more than a fragment, for more than a fragment of Time, after all—and only by seeing some slight aspect of the largeness of what it means to live here, now, in the fields of revelation, the courts of majesty, atop the mountains of joy . . . across the vast deserts of want. The needy kind of "want."

We are dwarfed, finally, and need-fully, by our resolute *finity*. By our opaque eyelids—by the way we blink when *Eternity* passes through our troubled air. It is too large a thing to look at; our retinas are eclipsed by such enormity. It is too much to embrace, to lift, to tote in our soul's small pocket, this Life within life. It has its grip upon *us*, of course.

Oh, but I want . . .

Ah, but my heart yearns . . . not always, nor even *often* for "toys and treasures," but for fine goals, worthy pursuits, fervently breathed hopes. For estimable attainments that waver on our soul's horizon. Please, God?

Is it unreasonable to ask God for favors—for things *we* would not necessarily grant us, were we God? For we know—oh, yes we do!—that God is not *daddy*, that his compassion is a flame that often sears, that licks against our pretensions of need until they are chars. Until their bare bones are revealed.

Until *my* bareness is laid before me.

And beneath this "proud flesh," my bones ache with the heat of *his* aching . . . for I have not asked for the only thing I need:

"Give me this day . . . "

Oh, grant me this simple hunger!

And so we are not small gods at all, after all—only children learning to divide and multiply, before the fish stinketh and the Bread dryeth. Learning "manners"—how to say *please and thank you*, learning how to wait before we grab.

How to stand, hands open, empty and unclutched.

The kitty leaves me for her happy hunting grounds. I leave my pencil and paper unattended, stretch my inert spirit, and sit poised, nose to the Wind, following my Hunger.

❧ ❧ ❧

A geranium spills over the end of the porch, thrusting its many awkward arms helter-skelter, wanting to lean, I guess.

Now a hummingbird zigzags across it, with its little wind-whipped "birrr" sound.

It is the common hummer—gray with a wash of iridescent red and green. *Common?* Every hummer is a jewel spinning on invisible filament— a gift to remind us of the preposterous delicacy which God has lavished upon his world.

Papa loved hummingbirds. When he could do little else in his final, frail years, he sat on his small back porch where a hummer family fanned back and forth to the feeder we had hung for them, for him. He recognized that preposterous Lavish of Creation with a depth I *now* recognize. Papa was not an orthodox believer. He was a cerebral and practical professor, but had a bent toward trout-fishing or birthing a lamb. Toward stooping to gather eggs and pick peas before his first class of the day.

How did *I* know that the glory of a speckled trout was the iridescence of a hummer's wings? I never looked, in those days.

Today is my father's birthday. *Was* his birthday. He is gone, no longer hunched from the struggle to breathe. I think his lungs are full of Glory, his eyes clear and a-feast on iridescence.

My parents lived with us for eight years—my father for six and a half of them, my mother lingering for another eighteen months. It was a hard stretch for the last four years. For all of us. This is one of the times in my life I'd hate to repeat, and yet dearly wish I could—on one level—with *hindsight*.

"Honor thy father and thy mother."

"He who loves father and mother more than me . . ."

We do not *naturally* explore the range of sacrificial love—love of God and love for others; we come to this unwitting and unwillingly. Our emotional and spiritual clumsiness ill-prepares us for such rough distractions and their fine distinctions. All too often we lose our boundaries and find ourselves entrapped.

How do we become, or remain, integrated beings when others pull at us beyond their failing comprehension? How do we recognize *our* own failing comprehension? *How do we love when the "noun" of it often becomes simply an "action verb"—the hard, daily doing of a commitment, a commandment, a promise "never to let go"?*

We live these lessons in the crucible. I doubt that we learn as much from our sweet successes, our triumphs of loving, as from our failures—or spotty performances. The *stoop-and-rise-and-stoop* of living instructs us in humility, helps us recognize the tally of the daily dole and purposes of Grace . . . which, ultimately is *his* triumph over our spotty natures.

Well, these spots have been rubbed raw, rubbed clean, rather like the abrading of a critical burn before it can re-flesh. God scourges, balms, heals all things. God forgives and delivers us daily—from our frailties and our strongholds. God redeems what *we* cannot relive and recover and replenish.

And we are given Sight. I see now what I could not see until now—that for all these recent years I had not finished my mourning and my healing. It is good *now* to be here, in a place my father would love, as plain as the soul of that educated son of the soil. It is good to be his child and *his* child, to cry one more time for losses too deep to name, and to find them attended . . . well attended.

It is well with my soul.

It is very good indeed to stand here looking out over this land that is not mine, finding it, possessing it somehow. God has been good . . . he sets before me now, *today*, my papa's natal-day, a hummer!—a perfect miniature of Glory, whirring at the tip of His finger. Against the backdrop of this homely porch and my homely soul!

Happy, happy birthday, Papa! Thank you for sharing it with me.

Here, upon me, a gray cat splurges, her throat extravagant with small and fluent rumblings, and if my soul could make such sound, I would, I would!

Vesla the kitty has been closed up all weekend. For her this is a prison, for me a sanctuary. For those here who work on projects world-wide, it is a pivot point, the hinge that swings their doors, that overlays or undergirds their ties with life. For Bea, it is a beloved creation of her making, a refuge that is perhaps becoming a burden.

Vesla and I are somewhat akin. Hemmed in, closed in by circumstances, we are let out to play for these few brief days. I open the door for her, as he does for me.

Like me, Vesla hesitates. In the dim house is security, her sustenance, a sunny table upon which to view life, a friendly neighbor who breaks up the day each day. Outside is the magic of nature, and its dark side. She knows the howl of coyotes and the territorial rights of the other ranch cats. It is *safer* inside, and she has grown used to solitude, to her cozy imprisonment.

We proceed to the front porch immediately. Only if I leave the door ajar does she relax at first. She spends much time going in and out, passing from security to freedom and back to her comforts again. Finally, an hour or so later, she is at peace on the porch, or beyond in a far patch of sunlit dust.

I *do* go in and out of my Father's house in such a way. I confess it almost reluctantly, for there are those (few) who call me *steadfast*. Yes, but—steadfast intent, unsteady practice!

All right, so we live in two worlds, and we do think of other things than Heaven, right?

That's not what I mean. The Kingdom of God isn't, I'm *sure it isn't,* being super-spiritual all day long, or I beg off. I'm not even interested!

I think, rather, that the Kingdom of Heaven is an *attitude* of *there,* or *here,* which permeates all our why's and wherefores. It is, maybe, a preamble to what we do, and say, and respond *to* and *as.* We acknowledge this, this here-there, by some interior Instinct implanted when we first said "Yes!" We discern, by our new nature, just where we are—what Ground we stand upon—and trust that the ground*ing* we step out upon will hold firm.

We cannot talk of *knowing* God without speaking of, and moving into and out of, his frame of reference. His domain or dominion. If we know him, as we are *known,* we are not admitting merely "I know *of* him." We know *of* many people, including presidents and princesses, and we know them only by repute and quote and a lot of hearsay.

Many of God's own people (Let's be honest now—that includes *very* many of us!)"know" him no more than this, never realizing the intimate, fluid relationship that this King of kings yearns to maintain with us "commoners," us earth-dwellers. Many of us, admitted believers in the Son of God, granting—even reverencing—the irrefutable historicity *of* this King, and knowing those who "know him" well, still choose to stand back, preferring the familiarity of our own domain to his dominion.

It isn't safe, this Promised Land of his, because it isn't visible, and it demands a leap across a frontier of faith. We play by humanity's rules, and lose what we have never Found.

God does leave his door ajar. We all come and go, truth be told. The door won't swing shut forever if we step out and smell the garbage and roll in the dust a bit. The Premises that we stand upon are real enough that they will not disappear, like Brigadoon, into some misty unreality for too long a season.

But every time we step beyond his province and provision, we negate the thought, the act, of God for this developing moment. *This* eternal Now! We miss the instant, the spark of conception—the Immaculate Conception of Intent which our Father proposes, which *is* the whole concept of the Kingdom, in a mustard-seed. Where miracles are conceived.

We shall not lose all by our losses. Here, in the Kingdom, the water does not flow only from the fountain of youth. I grow older every day; sometimes it startles me, but not others. The heart tells us more of Time than the calendar. In the Kingdom I am young and vigorous and full of pledge and promise, as I will forever be. If . . . if I choose and choose and choose.

The kitty rubs against me, seeking something more than food. Contact, companionship, assurance, security, freedom. A few words and strokes, and off she goes, smelling a smell or hearing some sound worth investigating.

Vesla is tamed by forces and persons beyond her control, even as we. Ah, yes! Life has nudged us into our neediness, our particular dependencies. Our whiskers twitch, you might say, at different stimuli. But, like Little One, we are tracking what is ours, in and out of the doors to our own small soul-room. We enter and are prone to leave—with small, nibbling doubts and desires and habits that goad and guide us. Or consume us . . .

Vesla is not free in her temporary freedom any more than we. We are bound to our necessities; some urge us on, some pull us back. My greater need, now—here, on this day given—may not be relevant to you. Or even to me, one day soon. But our *Need* beyond, or embracing all needs, is for something firm and fluid and coherent that will shape or reshape whatever happens to us. It is impossible to anyone but God, who replenishes our myriad possibilities as daily Bread.

This it is we feed upon; this it is that satisfies our hunger and makes us ever ravenous for more. The kitty comes back to me over and over, seeking more than food—for her bowl is not empty.

Truly we cannot live by bread alone. When we have walked beyond that Gate and found life stale and tasteless, we are welcomed back within. The Key is in the lock.

❧ 4 ❧

Ochre, dun, amber

THERE IS SOMETHING NEW in the way the sun enfolds the earth today. The harshness is gone. Or perhaps—*probably*—it has been me, my harshness. I don't want to spoil the delicacy of this gift by examination. This warmth is full of Presence.

There is a Fire which does not singe.

And something is happening within that has no antecedent. I have no known reason to feel this lightness, this *all-is-well* that wells up. It is unfamiliar; it is unearned, unbidden.

"You will go out in joy, and be led forth in peace; the mountains and the hills will burst into song before you, and all the trees of the field will clap their hands . . . . "

" . . . and let it begin with me." It begins now. It is Time.

I believe it now, this suddenness that has no context I have ever known. *I believe, yes!* Something unnamable has happened. Something of *Beyond*, where origins and endings recur daily, by the moment, splayed and splashed before my dull eyes, my muffled hearing.

Oh, let it begin and begin and begin again! I am so hungry for "it."

The whisper of the universe, the *I AM* that girdles and engulfs me, that separates me out from emptiness, that tortures and taunts the finity of my flesh . . . ah, it is this which must convince me, or I shall never know *peace*.

Remind me again, Creator of all that sings and soars and strives against our striving! Remind me again, oh Crucifier, that the Cross is not a stick that I shake at life as it passes.

The Cross is—shall ever be—the pivot-point, the certain summation of the Universal come before me.

It is Jacob's ladder, one great step, one high rung, one solid strut. There I may climb with angels. Stretch me, oh God!

Life sings and soars here, on this summer morning, with its newborn clarity. And every tree in this small Kingdom Come stands newly revealed before me, each awkward cruciform, in imitation and intimation of his being. In invitation of his coming.

Clap your hands, oh trees!

ॐ ॐ ॐ

Now and again we catch a glimpse of eagles in the back country. On much of the continent, including this county, they are rather a rare breed. I have seen only one here-about, some years ago, but then I am a "townie," and eagles need a largeness not of humanity's making.

Today I was preoccupied with small things—the uncertain shape of my life, the trail of crumbs that I had left behind for others, the losses stacked like unread books against my walls.

And then I saw *them*, two of them, each a phoenix rising high against the lowering sun! They made much of the wind, leaping from current to current, their pinions straining, flexing.

It was sport; they were not hunting. They labored upward, rather like oarsmen, heaving their sleek bodies through the stiffened air. At the apogee, they poised in equilibrium for one breathtaking moment. And then, and then they glided—oh, lovely! Gathering the air beneath them, they slipped down long invisible corridors, out, out across the mesa!

Masters of maneuver!

Far above, a military jet angled against the sun, leaving its detritus on the wind like smoke signals.

Pilots and eagles. My husband was once a Navy jet pilot. These men worked as hard at their intricate [war] games as the eagles I watched today—challenging the machines, gravity, each other, thrusting up and down the trackless sky. There was an excitement, a sense of mystery and yes, mastery that claimed them wholly. Nothing else was quite like this thrill that they alone knew.

A rare breed. They had their own language, their own criteria for what they did or didn't do, their own *mystique*. They were spoiled for lesser things, for the mundane thrills of the earth-bound. Of course each and all eventually came down to earth. Safely, I must add. And each and all became "normal"—discovered other visions, other ways of seeing. But never has a one of them forgotten the thrill of the flight.

The wings of an eagle. . .

I have often envied the Apostle Paul his mysterious trip to Heaven. How can we possibly imagine what he saw? Watching the eagles at play, I want suddenly to join them, join *him*. My most fervent prayers are for an eye to see far, far beyond what my small myopia affords. The *eye* of an eagle. I am ruined for my old ways . . . for small, tight summations, for narrow comprehensions. The world is too large to break into such a crumble of smallnesses!

Above the earth, soaring on his raft of hollow bones and feathers, the eagle sees everything both larger and smaller. But an eagle is an eagle is an eagle, forever hedged to the underside of Heaven.

And humanity is ever human. Soaring on wings of shaped metal does not grant vision unless the yearning for it was carried *into* the stratosphere. Vision comes to us most often when we have been in cramped and crowded places, where the walls have caved in and pressed us to our knees.

It comes with the rising, a moment of apogee.

This is a place of Sabbath. Horizon lines stretch out and ease from jagged up-and-down to slanted hills; their surfaces are carved in ochre, dun, amber. Between them, the long, gray snake of road hisses faintly in its man-made trench.

Sky Mesa Ranch . . . . It didn't register initially that when I came up here I was seeking, even yearning, albeit a bit vaguely, to leave my own small self behind—to understand what no human mind can fathom adequately: the Kingdom of God. What I have learned in, yes, a primal way is: the mind does not get me there. I was *already there*, here, in a sense. Of course! I never understood those "Aha!" moments, those engulfing, shivering other-world sensations, the inexplicable way complexities unraveled before my stuttering thoughts could quite reweave them. I knew how to parse a poem, but never, no never, had I learned the dialect of God. Never, by conscious thought, had I unearthed the Edenic from the clay and shale of life. Until now.

I suddenly saw, from the porch out over the yard, a new landscape. I perceived the incomprehensible—that what I had entered into was a metaphor too viable, too startling to dismiss. I had been planted here expressly for this reason—to catch a glimpse of that Greater Kingdom by looking through the smudged lens of this smallish acreage. Everywhere I looked, the parallels unrolled, drawing me on and in. For me, the Kingdom of Heaven and Sky Mesa are, at this moment, come together.

I think I have entered a new place. Something has changed within me that causes change in what I perceive around me.

It is a long time coming. But here *it* is; without fanfare or proclamation *it* has come to me—that *"it"* I stammered over a few short weeks ago. So simply, like the Word whispered to Elijah. Now I can begin to hear it, to speak it, speak of it. Now I can learn to pray it, invoke it, yearn over it, with all my misplaced yearnings!

The Kingdom is elusive; God made it that way. We know so little about it that it becomes merely a parable about parables, a list of "ingredients" that Christ listed at another time about another place. So we miss it; it passes us by, by our default.

I always had a problem with the Kingdom of Heaven. It was too far from me to wonder about, much less *worry* about. I secretly thought, in my early years, that the Kingdom of God/Heaven was a sort of LaLa Land— Pie-in-the-Sky, Further-over-the-Rainbow. Ah, but now that I *see* it, I see it everywhere. It is created, sight by sight, behind our opened eyes.

Such a Wind-sweeping move from our rubble and stubble into a realm of clean-swept concepts and precepts is staggering! It is awe-full, meeting God on Holy ground! Holy *becomes*. It once was a remote four-letter word that chilled our secret fevers; now we say it with stammering tongues, our throats all husky with unpronounceable joy.

Freedom is Holy, is beautiful with all the beauty of pure intent, of passion that has caught flame from the compassion of God. Here abideth faith, hope, love. And God's unimaginable self. Here, descending in some manifest and unseen way, is manifest, unseen Presence. The Creator wraps his cloaks and courts around him and settles the Kingdom upon our very dust!

Like Jesus on the road to Emmaus, he walks unrecognized. Christ incognito, a Breath beyond our own labored breath, a Heart-pulse beneath our own.

This is his Kingdom we step into, all unknowing, like a tousled child into a Secret Garden. We know him by the Hush within us which is full of Sounding, like that which a ship makes in the deeps. We *know*: this is what Home is.

His Kingdom *is* come, is *coming* . . . Eternal Now. On this smallish porch I find him waiting in the morning mist, pointing out beyond the hills and valleys, out beyond this Sky Mesa. He *sees*, and my eyes squint to catch the reflection. It is time to *do* something, together.

Now I am faced with an impossible goal—of giving words to the inexpressible, the indefinable. How long—how cautiously—have I skirted around the edge of this vision, not daring to test it, much less pursue it?

The Kingdom of God *is* coming! It has been a long time coming! I can scarcely interpret that great Obsession which has gripped far greater minds than mine these past 2000 years—but that doesn't matter, not at all. If I say well enough something well worth saying, it will be less a redundancy than a soul-felt *amen*.

God used an ass once to make a speech well worth making. I'm sure Linda the donkey could tell us something important if given a mandate. But I am "mandated" to hitch up my serape and explore the Kingdom.

That's reason enough to begin again each day.

ə♥ ə♥ ə♥

This morning I walked along the periphery road, camera in hand. I snapped pictures and plucked up a bounty of drying weeds and found a small bone—remnant of a fox or coyote long since gone.

My weed-find was purple sage. A week ago they were passing into bud—long, stiff stalks rising majestically above the mother plant. Today the aroma engulfs me as I approach. The lavender blossoms are open, their contrast with the pale turquoise leaflets as striking as any hot-house bouquet. Roses would be incongruent here.

As I hiked the border of the property, a woman waved at me from one of the lovely new homes in the carved-out hillside just beyond. I waved back, wishing we could walk together. We inhabit two different worlds right now, although her world is just a bit nearer my own daily reality. Every time she looks out her large picture windows she sees Sky Mesa huddled beyond her, with its small clutter of buildings and sheds. She has never been here, and perhaps is only vaguely curious about this rather disheveled spread.

But so it is, so often: we look across fences at each other, perhaps even wave or smile. We humans are often a genial lot, and apt to wish each other well. But we are not apt to *climb* fences unless the grass is distinctly lusher beyond us. Her grass *is* lusher, her small kingdom lovely. And I have here a wealth she, perhaps, cannot imagine.

Sky Mesa is a heart-wealth. The old rock pump house brings up cool water faithfully, even in extended drought. The water is far better than what my neighbor drinks. Water out of a rock! I fill my large jug every day, and one for Bea. It is a source of unceasing reassurance.

In the near distance, remnants of fog cling to the hills and soften their harshness. Through a veiled face we see God. Through the dark glass of our picture windows, we peer at the Kingdom of God. What we see is far less than what is there.

We live at tangents to each other, touching now and again, brushing sleeves and thoughts, sometimes "rubbing each other up" or rubbing raw. To a large extent, it's simply the result of being one human in a world crammed with our kind. We can't relate to everyone, or, on a significant, personal level, more than a few.

But Jesus did. Of course! He was God enfleshed. We're not; not by a mile—or a universe. Well, no. But he did say something startling about us and him and his Father, *to* his Father. It was in that last, long message-cum-prayer before Gethsemane. He told it precisely as it is—or is meant to be.

"As you sent me into the world, I have sent them into the world."

Sometimes I think we have never really heard him. I *mean* to hear him. Finally.

ع ع ع

A donkey lives here. Linda is a sag of bones and ripple of tired muscle and thatch of unkempt pelt. Linda is a belly that looks ready to burst with foal; she is as old in donkey-years as Sarai was to Abraham, and her womb is long empty. Linda is two rheumy eyes that beg for something she cannot name and I cannot give. Linda leans with a sigh against the uncertain fence, or against my unfamiliar hand, and my heart aches. It is, perhaps, foolish to love a donkey so—and so quickly. But I am often foolish.

When I watch Linda, I am always struck by her patience. Donkeys are traditionally "temperamental." Not so, not here! Linda lost her mate last winter. Surely the beasts of the field know grief and loneliness; I see it in her eyes. Perhaps it is this that gives her an air of quiet grace. That's an unusual statement to make of a donkey—especially one with as broken-down a chassis as this one.

Somehow this gives me consolation—sharing this time and place with her. There is such a separation between human lives, the processes of getting along, getting ahead, getting by—and the natural world, that which we call *wild,* which struggles on, much too tangential to our own.

We see a flash or so of the other "order" in our passages between our life experiences, or perhaps more likely, when these experiences wane. We may dote upon the pets around our feet (and they are often vital, life-enriching—and sometimes, perhaps our *stead,* our alter egos), but for most of us the breadth of the animal world exists mainly behind bars and barriers of place and purpose.

We cannot, by our minimal exposure, know the great heart of an elephant. Learn patience from the patterning of a covey of quail. Explain the explicit cosmos of the bee. We see too little value in the furry and feathery denizens of this planet, other than admiring their occasional beauty or oddity. Or granting our continual and anonymous picking clean of the bones of the edible.

But I see the incarnate here, in this old gray lady-beast. An embodiment laid firmly, consciously, upon the earth-life all around me. In Linda's gaunt dignity I am reminded of the promised Child who was carried lightly upon her once, the fullness in his mother's womb.

I see the sorrow of the man-Christ, the weight of his burden for Jerusalem, for humanity . . . and how the weight of us all has bowed the back of this beast of burden.

It is not unkind to ride a donkey. But humanity has ridden too far, too long, on the back of nature, and has never reached Jerusalem.

Linda is "only" a beast, a domesticated animal rummaging at the fence-edge, at the far edge of a long and well-lived life.

When she leans her frowzy head against me, Christ weeps with us both.

And I would give life back to her, if it were my gift to give.

The old gray and white goose roams freely throughout the orchard.

Annie is at least ten years old, and has made her rounds day after day, following her imprinted nature and the experiences life has brought to her.

Inevitably she comes to rest next to the chicken yard fence and wallows in the shade and dust, to preen and observe. She does not want *in* the pen; the others do not seem to want out. Hennish and goosey minds run on parallel tracks in many ways, but their "fowl behavior" does not make them clones.

Watching the goose shuffle down into her crater next to the fence, I can't help thinking of the envy which has gripped me for a lifetime. It still nibbles at me. How surreptitious it is! How *nagging*! How high a fence it becomes to my starving soul. I have often failed to see it in myself; less rarely do I miss it in others as I've grown all too familiar with the ways of the world. (The concept that we most dislike those traits in others that mirror our own flaws is probably true.)

I must confess this: I have yearned for treasures buried in other folks' fields (Matt. 13). No, none of us is innocent of such envy. It is not their toys I want, but their impetus, their inner *persuasion of purpose*, maybe. The single-hearted-mindedness that "it takes" to "succeed." A hard quality to pin down, a shifting anchor in those murky waters of desire.

For years I struggled to fit myself into the fairly flexible perimeters of our local and national Christian writers' guilds. A dear and devout and fluid gang of word-mongers, we were sincerely and often effectively dedicated to shaping and sharing the Gospel, and our experiences of it, to meet varied needs of the larger Christian community. *And*, of course, hoping to touch others who might find hope in our witness. A worthy articulation, and the Gospel would be dis-hearted if it were not for such timeless, ongoing testimony from his scribes. These were my "significant others," with good reason: integrity, purpose, abiding faith . . . and that Love which invites and confirms. They still remain bedrock in my life.

But . . . a large "but." All this goodness beside and around and beyond me could not mend my flaw. My basic, if not secret, *unfaithfulness*: I did not write from *who I am*, but shaped myself awkwardly into *who I wished I were, or "should be."* My words often dangled in mid-air. They hid inscrutably in dark corners. They lay as deflated as a football kicked too many times. I was a mimic, a mime. I coveted the way these expositors had of paring down his sacred Logo into articles and editorials and life experiences that graced the pages of our sometimes excellent journals of faith. And, *oh yes!*—even into books—the ultimate goal of each of us.

I never fully sought, nor embraced this person struggling within who had a voice all her own. I wanted, quite simply, to be someone I was not. The curse, perhaps, of the human race.

Other things happened inside me that kept intercepting all the "Good Works" I forged. I felt vaguely dysfunctional often, out of the flow and dry with longing. Right there, in the midst of all these wonderful, and still wonderful, writing companions, I felt . . . disjointed. Dishonest. Because, yes, in one crucial way, I was. My burnt offerings were true, were Gospel, and were someone else's privilege and priority. I was a poet in the garb and guise of a teller of Truth, a purveyor of faith.

"This above all: to thine own self be true, and it must follow, as the night the day, thou canst not then be false to any man." The Bard, of course. Great *para*phras*er* of Truth.

Never mind that "they" sometimes oohed or aahed over my frequent poetic meanderings. Never mind that poetry is a worthy distillate of all I saw, yearned for, believed in . . . all I wanted to stand for. I was, simply put, not on quite the same Journey, and I always felt it heart-deep. *But they were my people!* I knew that heart-deep, too! They were not the problem; I was. I wanted what they "had." I was willing, ready, to forfeit something intensely personal to be fully one of them.

One day, meeting at my house, a precious sister looked up from my handout (the worksheets we passed around to critique), her brow a bit furrowed, and said to me, gently, *"Have you ever heard of the KISS principle?"* I shook my head, puzzled. Quietly, distinctly, and unforgettably—she smiled gently to mitigate the ouch-factor: *"Keep It Simple, Stupid."*

Ouch. But she was absolutely right. I had shaped my own best attempt to fit what I can only describe as someone else's voice—their "enduement." His Way for me lay a bit off-center, and by struggling to be their jogging/jotting companion in the race (as brother Paul enjoins), I missed the seemingly narrow Path set before me.

I was Dorothy on the yellow brick road. Yes, even *There*, on the Way of the Master Wordsmith of all time. Called to write, undeniably—and as I much later discovered, irrevocably. Forever *wondering*. And wandering, always wandering. I was lost and had no coherent concept of how near Home was.

The ache, the bruise of this has haunted me far too long. It has been a hindrance simply because I saw it so. Standing here on this aging porch, watching the witless fowl peck and scratch endlessly, I see the witless pattern of my own scratching. Pecking at life.

And this I see with new clarity: in the Peaceable Kingdom, my resolution—my own sacred Journey—depends less upon parsing the natural endowments, the patterns of humanity, than on exploring *his*. His surprising, eloquent, plainspoken MindSet that permeates and penetrates all that is, overwhelming anything of lesser scope:

His Mind, *Set.*

A shaving, a crumble, a chip off the nature of *I AM*, the unspeakable Essence . . . who is, yes, forever speaking.

And this I see as well: I never lived as who *I am*, not fully, not really. The writing was just a part of my defection. For a lifetime I have deferred to other people's visions, their view of life, their yea's and nays and ways—yes, wanting to honor them and, well, wanting to absorb something missing in me.

There's a time for each of us to re-enter our core of life . . . to pick up the pieces we left behind in all our scratching for substance, for sustenance. His Gift to us each: the Mind of Christ. Treasure of another sort, a work of both heart and art. I know this; I have always *known* it, if peripherally. I must simply ask *him* to embed it. Lest I try (for the umpteen hundredth time) to limit God, and my chicken-little self, to my own skewed assessment.

The difference is all the difference in the world.

ᘐ   ᘐ   ᘐ

Growing up during and after a world war taught me thrift, taught me make-do. Taught me to glean and gather and yes, hoard. I was too young to understand the whole dynamic of self-denial for a greater cause. Of the difference between "want" as noun of barren necessity and verb of deep desire.

There was no distinguishing, in my child-eye, the gulf between an absence of jelly beans at the neighborhood store and Papa's car up on blocks for lack of gas and rubber. When a rare order of candy showed up, I stood in line with every kid from blocks around. We didn't share a bite. We hid our tiny treasures carefully.

And I learned all too well the principle of saving—the principle of *concealing as a virtue*, whatever the substance. My peanuts and my poems. It parched my soul somehow—a drought I could not recognize . . . and I brought this desiccation into my faith journey. Searching for oases, searching for hidden water, searching a long desert trek I charted without a glance upward.

No manna. No daily bread of Heaven.

And so. And so I am here to learn and unlearn, in reverse. *To trust in chickens? As chickens do?* Perhaps. To discern those things and issues that do, or do not, warrant trust. To trust in the timeless replication of spring and autumn, not the weather and all the whethers that define its permutations.

To *skeptically* cherish the nature of humanity and my own stained soul. To fathom, albeit dimly, the nature of God—and the great noun "want," and how my desires have verbed a consuming "need" within. How my intentions betray me, belay me. And oh, yes!—finally and ever—finding and cherishing and living out what is intrinsically meant to be mine, by his intent.

My turf. My troughs and wallows. Whatever acreage is mine to homestead, to plow, enjoy, struggle with. My work, un-work, poverties, privileges—to accept each as down payment on his Kingdom, to learn to be faithful. For a day and a lifetime. To genuinely *treasure* whatever treasures I find, too long buried in my rubbled earth, my genes, my history. Whether great or small—a source of wonder or promise to others who see much come from little, or little fuss made over muchness.

I know, gut-deep, it is not an exercise in futility, a rosy-glow promise, an over-the-rainbow construct. It has to be the most practical aspect of my embedded faith: ongoing trust in him who has promised to be with me, to give me each day my daily Bread.

It is his plot I till, his plots I work out. The yield comes with toil both of the hands and the Spirit, always. With the mulch of creativity and the water of compassion. What springs forth is after its own kind, my kind as *he* chooses it, cloned and seeded off a corner of his great Thought, a match fitted to my own imprinted nature. It lives and it thrives, and it multiplies.

By his great, inimitable replication. Only, and always.

❧ 5 ❧

The Kingdom unfolds, unrolls

It is early afternoon, and I am lolling back in the rocker, playing with my coffee cup and watching the small, enclosed chicken yard on the far side of the orchard. A beautiful cock of variegated color struts up and down, keeping order, reminding the varied residents in his small kingdom where they belong.

Cockadoo is much aware of what happens within his domain. A stranger like me is ignored unless I should pick up either a feed bucket or an egg basket. He is aware of what transpires beyond the fence only if it "registers" on his personal index of relevancies: Critter approaching (move to center). Missus approaching (act hungry), etc.

The world is full of "Cockadoo's." We are *all* Cockadoo's, in a sense. *I* am most certainly Cockadoo, species-/gender-transformed. I can only respond to so much, and it must be relevant, or I lose my grip on life.

There is a lot of relevant life going on outside Cockadoo's pen, but his idea of relevant is highly rooster-ish. What I respond to is highly people-ish. Or *person*-ish. It is based on too many factors to calculate, but inevitably I respond according to what I have taught myself regarding life. Not necessarily simply what *life* has taught, for the same life circumstances presented to six people would produce six variations on "what life has taught." We react; ergo we create—new circumstances.

When, like Cockadoo, I ignore certain things and fix on others, it is because some things are necessarily or seemingly relevant, and some aren't. *And*, like our fowl friend, some seem one and are the other. A hatchet in hand may not look menacing to Cockadoo—not until it is too late! And a hungry "varmint" outside his fence would seem very menacing, for Cockadoo's brain does not compute the concept "fence" as well as the smell of *varmint*.

41

Ah, and m*e*? I am, of course, fenced in by life in numerous ways. All of us are fenced in. We see ourselves as victims or free spirits, or more likely somewhere on that sliding scale between. We spend our life trying to control our responses, fitting them as best we can to the matter at hand. But we are circumscribed by circumstances both within and beyond us—both too often beyond our conscious control.

"There is a way which seemeth right . . . ."

Our "good ideas" too often fleece us; they keep us warm for a season; they pull the wool over our eyes finally.

God has Vision. We don't. He sees a larger grace of living for each of us at any given moment, at every Given moment. We scarcely perceive what that means to us, for we have become so used to the known perimeters of our thoughts, our pinched circumstances, our habits and responses, and those of our significant (and *in*significant) others. Cockadoo has a lot to tell us here!

And what he tells me, in a strange new way, a small and infinite metaphor, is becoming a reality I have too long ignored:

The Kingdom . . . it is the Kingdom of God we crave.

God breaks down our fences and stakes out new territory. What that means to you and to me are two quite different things. He may uproot your life in a dramatic way, and simply grant me a vital new perception of what is *possible*, right where I am. But oh, the territory is his, and he transforms everything, everything! He *must*.

That is because, of course, when God brings down his Kingdom, pulls it over our sheepish eyes, unfolds it across our parched perceptions, it is suddenly our Promised Land—a place of Promise, a promising place to dwell in.

Here. Now.

The Kingdom comes differently to us all, as well—and differently at different times. Tomorrow is a new territory to explore, and the Kingdom will include adventures and dilemmas, joy and pain we cannot foresee or perhaps could not even respond to today.

A few months ago I taped two small quotes onto my computer frame and into my writing notebook. I knew they were significant; my yearning over them was enormous. Now I understand—in a way I could not perceive then.

> "*Discovery is seeing what everybody has seen and thinking what nobody has thought.*" Albert Szent-Gyorgyi

"The only real voyage of discovery consists not in seeking new landscapes but in having new eyes." Marcel Proust

Where God has stepped and stopped, there is Life beyond smallness and pain and confusion and despair and hate and diffidence! Our passions and dispassions are consumed in Fire too great to resist, and they burn with a new wick, fed by an oil we never knew.

The Kingdom unfolds, unrolls, laid across a world we have loathed and loved, despaired of and despoiled, and there is no stopping it.

It comes because our Creator promised his Land to us.

❧ ❧ ❧

Annie Goose can see the full trough of food within the chicken yard. Her own bowl has been empty for half a day. The chicken brood can certainly see tempting morsels scuttling along right outside their peripheries.

But it *is* peaceful. Neither Annie nor Cockadoo and his ladies seem to be complaining of their lot in life. Their life patterns are well set. They *know* the hand that feeds them and they know Bea will appear, on time, just as she always has. It is sufficient for them to know that what is theirs will come to them when they need it.

It reminds me of Jesus' words about lilies and sparrows. Unto each its own, for this day. *Day unto day unto day, his provision comes—in the form which he discerns best.*

This is a hard statement to accept. And yes, hard to "prove" in a way that convinces the spiritual skeptic.

The foundational realities of faith are first *discerned*—and, ultimately, learned. Not the reverse. *No one can convince us to believe the unbelievable.* Or how to know what it is, of course. This is the function, the "preoccupation" of the Holy Spirit—that indefinable, indefatigable Witness (for want of a better word) of God-Being-with-us.

To put it in simplistic, and yes, clumsy terms (as always, no matter how *anyone* attempts to explain the incomprehensible), I reckon the Person of the Holy Spirit functions as controller of the "light switch." We will never find a metaphor to illuminate the incalculable manifestations of God-Being-with-us, so we'll leave the light switch.

But without that deliberate, all-powerful and immediate and/or incremental flood of comprehension, of fathoming somehow the unfathomable, the *unreasonable*—of knowing with no innately human way of knowing . . . we are clueless.

We are all, at some point in life, sidelined by an accumulation of opinions we have gathered, attitudes that "make sense" to us, dismay at all the half-baked spiritual "truths" that melt in the heat of reality. Much of what we "know" is perhaps "educated" (that is, studied and stewed upon) but it invariably ends up as chaff. Cerebral dandruff. It proves to be psychological detritus simply because that's not where faith begins, or ends.

While our mind is chock full of suppositions, *it is our spiritual cupboard that is dim, is bare,* and we generally don't realize it *is* bare. Because, as Paul says, we "see through a glass darkly." For lack of Light.

We don't flip the switch; *he* does. He knows when, why, and how. He knows, to begin with, whether we even *want* light. He knows the nature of our darkness and when to "invade" it—when we are weary of fighting our demons, fighting those of others, fighting for foothold. He knows when and whether our "perfect offering" is, indeed, dandruff.

We are, even the wisest among us, futile and sometimes fatuous. And when the "lights go off," we are helpless without him.

Jesus reminded his disciples that he must go, and that the Father would send his Holy Spirit to tell us all we need to know. We can only stand beckoning—beaconing, if you will—watching, waiting for a trickle or burst of revelation, yearning for discernment, recognition. Accepting—no, *begging* a vast humility that opens the pores of faith.

And yes, he will appear, on time, just as he always has. The One who teaches.

The cracks in the structure of life are where we find him. It is sufficient.

≈ ≈ ≈

Thus we are granted amnesty and certain amenities. Our turf. Our troughs and wallows. Whatever "acreage" is ours to homestead, to plow, enjoy, struggle with. Our work, our un-work, our poverties, our privileges—accepting all as down payment on his Kingdom. Learning to be faithful, for a day and a lifetime. May whatever treasures we find, too long buried in our rubbled earth, soon or late become great or small—a source of wonder and joy or, yes, reluctant revelation to others who see so much come from such a little, or so little fuss made over such a muchness. It is not an exercise in futility, a rosy-glow promise, an over-the-rainbow construct. It is the most practical aspect of our embedded faith: ongoing trust in him who has promised to be with us, to give us each day our daily Bread.

It is his plot we till, his plots we yearn for. The yield comes. With toil both of the hands and the Spirit, always. With the mulch of our creativity and the water of our compassion. What springs forth is after its own kind, cloned and seeded off a corner of his great Thought, a match fitted to our own imprinted nature. It lives and it thrives, and it multiplies. By his great, inimitable replication. Only and always.

Whether we need rain or grain, his Provision is beyond our own determining, and if we observe rainclouds forming over our small, desiccated plots and do not see it as provision, or trust in his protection, it shall not be. If we see the grain as lifeless or meager, it is. But out of thunder and dust he created our fathomless universe and our unfathomed *being*. Out of such have *we* come forth. He wants to spoil us—yes, spoil us! —from living with any other mindset.

My corner of the Kingdom is not of *my* choosing, for my Father has unrolled it lovingly before me.

Whatever he perceives for my life is there—is *here, on my way to "there," wherever his "there" might be.* His "there" may change, depending on what I do with my present tense—my "here," but I can open my needy hands and greedy heart for what is mine; it is a greed and need too long misplaced.

Greed for God. It withers any lesser greed we had.

God's bounty? Oh, I want all of it, whatever it is! He can make me wise beyond a Doctorate, with a wisdom beyond my guarded mind. He can take this small income and an open heart and find creative ways of multiplying my generosity until I am wealthy in ways that the wealthy never know! I may be replete with all that I can grasp and let go of. And I will have learned it from him! This is perhaps the second-greatest Secret in the world, this continual flow of Grace—the first being the One who spilled the Secret for us. Amen.

All my early-strewn winter "rye" (perhaps "rue" is more accurate) has shriveled in the present heat—lifeless seed upon the dust of my ways. But he creates *green*. Life comes to me again and again from other than my plotting, and beyond me lie borders and pastures I know not of. What is mine tomorrow and tomorrow comes from whatever harvest I am promised, and what I do with it. Whatever I am promised is dealt, measure upon measure, in each moment's transaction. Open hand, open heart.

Annie Goose receives her corn and such from her mistress's hands, just as does Cockadoo. They live amicably side by side—the one cooped safely, the other dependently free. The old girl sits in her hollow of dust and waits for her handout and whatever stray bugs come her way, and she watches Cockadoo preen.

I think she looks a bit like me—not such a silly goose at all . . .

❧ ❧ ❧

A pair of white doves also roosts in the chicken yard, high above Cockadoo and his busy ladies, soothing and smoothing ranch life with their mellow reiterations. They groom themselves, and each other, and watch, with a patient eye, the small frenzies beneath them.

The metaphor here is too simplistic to play on for long. Suffice it to say that they live two different lives, on two planes—these lovely "birds of the air" and the landlubbers beneath. The Spirit and the flesh. Avians though they all are, they seldom interact, except perhaps over a stray morsel of life that wanders into the enclosure.

The continual squawks or honks from ground level create a varied counterpoint in the raucous symphony before me. The doves' plaintive repetitions do not dominate the environs, but are a thread tying it together—like a recurring descant, the steady theme of nature.

Perhaps their voice resembles somewhat the voice of God, which echoes over and over, unceasingly, above the din and cackle of our busyness, of our own incessant inner chatter. Do we *really* hear him? Perhaps we are deafened by the clang of other compelling sounds, or so used to ignoring that still, small voice that it becomes a "soothing background."

A modicum of praise; a mini-worship; a half-hearted medley of "yea and amen" is ours. Ah, but *"the mountains sing together for joy,"* and the doves pour their articulate peace upon me here, breaking great Silence with their two long, pure, descending syllables—breaking through the clatter beneath them with pure antiphony.

The chicken yard is always a blitz of great busyness. Why do these fowl always seem so *important* in their preoccupations? Full of "hustle and bustle" and instant commentary . . . an uncanny mimicry of us.

And the doves wrap their feet around their high perch and turn an occasional turn—and observe, often in silence. When they speak, their fluency seems far less a response to the small flutter beneath them than a commentary on life as they see it from where they rest. The philosophers of the brood.

For all their repetitiveness, the conversations of the doves are not intrusive, not assertive. When they say their say, it comes evenly, without fanfare, without a great flapping or a great flap. Then they settle back quietly once more, nuzzle a bit, groom a little, and resume their reflection on life beneath and beyond them.

It reminds me somehow of that rare quality we call humility. I am deeply drawn to humility, awed by *humble*.

We so often misjudge, for good or ill, the *being* of this state of being.

It has taken me much too long to figure out the real thing. Its decoys are so devious; we often mistake one for the other. Did he not say we are to be *"wise as serpents and innocent/guileless as doves?"* We get stuck in pursuing the first metaphor. It is a dangerous place. I know it well.

I too rarely examined my own particular "brand" of pride because it was not based upon the usual, normal things we covet, or envy toward the kind of people we often emulate. But it was always there, like a zit on the end of my nose, and I saw it in the mirror when I didn't have my guard up. I yearned to be above the clamor and clatter of pettiness*es* that betrayed him all around me. The dove in the chicken yard. "Goodness" was my God.

Ah, vanity above all vanities! Nobility? *I was far from it.* What I didn't seek was its father . . . purity. Its mother . . . meekness.

Real humility is obviously not self-conscious, as was *this* poor specimen of womanhood. But more to the point, it is not obsequious in any way, openly or covertly. Humble has a steady voice. I believe it knows its soul's worth before God; therefore it need not defend it, fight for it, insist upon it. The humble, I sense, can "be granted" such causes as I "yearned for," simply because they have conquered their own demons. Their strength lies in the pulse of God.

Humility doesn't really even know that it's humble. If it "knows," it ain't.

I wanted to be *noble!* —like John, the beloved, who, having leaned on *his* bosom, went on to write His message to the ages. Or like the centurion, who saw with such insight into his Kingdom, beyond the mud-flecked eyes of the disciples. Or St. Therese, who earned the (sometimes grudging) admiration and devotion of both sexes in a day when women were silent *or* silenced. Certainly Luther, who, risking death, banged the Law of Grace against the church's ramparts, and . . . yes, Mother Teresa in the gutters. Solzhenitsyn, who faced a tyrannical state virtually alone. And woke the

47

sleeping giant. Oh, and who but Nelson Mandela could have gone from prison to president!

Their *humble* fed my false humility . . . and I was blind to it! In part, because no one of them looked quite like the others, spiritually. They didn't wear an armband with a big "H" on it. I suspect that not a one of them measured themselves against the humble-cred of another. Humble is more like what you breathe out from that *pneuma* you have breathed in. It is the intangible essence of His pure intent. A response of unvaried purity in a wild variation of conditions.

The child-like trust of the young disciple John looked nothing like the disgust of Luther nailing his 95 theses to the church door, which was far removed from the little nun in Calcutta, holding the stinking bodies of the dying.

Breathing *pneuma* to them.

This I know, from years of attentive observation: the humble have great sensitivity; they recognize and acclaim or commend the often slender, hidden worth of others, and, when sin rears up before them, they find it easy to acknowledge their own frailty alongside that of others. Frailty made whole becomes their bridge, their hand outstretched. Henri Nouwen, another recent example, labeled this variable person: they are, each, the "wounded healer." Yes.

Oh, yes! By their mended frailties they are made whole. And with a bit of tongue-in-cheek humor (impossible with a forked tongue!) do they face life and their own rough agendas. I swear I can hear the doves chuckle! The humble neither crow nor cackle. I think they know how to laugh well and easily, though—at themselves. First and forever, at themselves!

Humility walks on bruised feet—but it does not limp.

Ah, and neither do the humble cripple others, for their own gain. "*The humble shall inherit the earth,*" he said. The humble alone know his power. They have the freedom of a certain distancing—a slight detachment from their own want, from that restlessness which forever strives and prods and plans. Oh, me!

The humble can perceive others with a certain Eye. They can be trusted with the soul of humankind, entrusted with the soul of nature. *And specifically, powerfully, with the nature of soul!* Ah, it is real humility that builds the unseen bridges between us. It takes that kind of strength. The power, the insight to build a walk-way for those who do not know the nature of *bridge.*

The humble are not wimps. Humility is the ultimate power.

Christ alone epitomized humility, of course. But now and then some of his children truly pick up on it. *Guileless* . . . Awesome, oh, it is awesome—beautiful! And both fleeting and enduring. The prick of pride always nibbles at humility, proclaiming its lies against truth.

I am not *there*. I'm merely on my journey toward understanding it. There are moments of clarity when the great Truth I live for becomes *all*—becomes a sudden opening in Eternity.

Me, Lord? Even me? I am *nothing* then, and yet, for that instant, the apple of his eye, and with David I cry out of his majesty. *Over and over and over again . . . .*

> *"My soul shall make its boast in the Lord.*
> *The humble shall hear it and be glad."*

Humbling, oh yes! Ah, and then back to daily*ness*. Pecking and scratching again. But, watching the doves, I am learning to settle back and look out at life. Nuzzle it a little. Cradle it now and then. Humble? Me? In all humility, I say "No!" A jest will do here.

The doves grip their perch with steady feet. I am not yet steady. But I *know humble* now. It comes from walking in Shoes too large for our own clumsy feet.

> *"As he who called you is holy, be holy." (*I Pet.1:15)

holy

> there are easier words than holy
> no illumining parables
> no enlightened discourse
> nor secret inclination
> nudge our struggling penchant into holy
>
> holy is historically so *Holy*
> evoking
> sacred blood-filled rituals
> corporal & corporate mystery
> invocations offered at our Hallowed Altars
> in high and vaulted temples
>
> But the word outstrips such
> heightened disembodiment

holy is
spare lean uncomely
unrobed
robbed of all royalty

like Jesus on his knees
clad foolishly in a diaper of sorts
ladling water over filthy feet

When we stumble awkwardly
tripping in our blinding desperation
when our vaulted souls yearn out
cry out teetering
groping for some kind of balance

ah holy

Oh, yes, we will learn to walk differently.

ॐ   ॐ   ॐ

✲ 6 ✲

To mend my raggedness

COCKADOO IS BLIND TO the size of Sky Mesa Ranch. He knows only his small territory. Annie Goose and Linda the donkey have a somewhat greater perception, but only because they are less confined. They are hemmed in by fences and their own beastie-brains.

My bit of Kingdom is smaller than I might have wished, and larger than I ever dreamed, lavish with Grace. He who framed my life has allowed me, like Annie Goose, to wander outside a cage I once dwelt in. Not very far out, for now; and my "cage" was a prison for only as long as I saw it so. So are all our cells (both meanings), whether one room or many, a marriage or none, poverty or a wretched past . . . or an illness that haunts our days.

Our inner landscape. We mostly live in "small places." But the Kingdom is as large as all Creation, beginning with the next step we take, the next thought we live in. In his territory, there is *"food ye know not of."*

Paul, great Kingdom kingpin, came out of an impeccable background in Tarsus and into impoverishment and danger. He told his friends in Philippi that he had learned the secret of Life: being content in any and every situation—hungry or full, rich or poor. Yes, I am frail, like Paul, and becoming newly strong. I will know Paul like a brother—*"His strength made perfect in my weakness."* Only a man who had survived his own holocaust could write that with perfect Strength.

Oh, yes, I am heading *there—not quickly, for it does not come quickly, this dance with God.* But it is the only safe place I know, the only Rest for running feet—where adventure multiplies to fit the soul's great need.

I am now, I insist, at his bidding. It becomes now his doing. I will fail and fail and he will bend and bend to my need, and walk me there. There, where failing is not failure.

In his Kingdom is Rest enough to mend my raggedness and send me searching (not *groping*) my way up life's mountains in spiritual boots. *There is, I know now, no level place.* I will not bound along at a good clip; there are too many rocks and hidden twists in the path. I will discover only the one step my foot must make, but my eyes can shift from path to panorama. I will be free to see the landscape.

I believe now that Vision isn't seeing the whole length of the path before me; it is seeing the step before me in the country around and beyond me. That has to make all the difference in my perspective. When I am "down and out," I know it is greatly due to my skewed perception of both "down" and "out." Corny, but true. And I am the church, in microcosm.

The church is surely meant to be his eye upon the world, his steady view into the Eternal, His *way* of walking among us. When I cannot see the glory and grandeur and gifting of God's endowment to his church, his people, and how it is ever laid upon a shattered world, I cannot know where I stand right now—I cannot perceive the holiness, the sacredness of *being* in that standing, in this place. In this fruitless, Godless, devious and devil-driven world we love.

When I cannot see this, as he does, I have no Vision.

And when I cannot perceive the hardship and pain and evil out beyond my door with real sensitivity, I do not have a large enough context for my own hardship, pain, and yes, evil. When I cannot respond to another's joy or goodness or wellness, I may cripple us both, and all my soul's *un*Certainties are a rubble set between us.

Who is blind but my servant, and deaf like the messenger I send? Who is blind like the one committed to me, blind like the servant of the Lord? You have seen many things, but have paid no attention; your ears are open, but you hear nothing. (Isa. 42)

Oh, grant us Vision, that we may see your Kingdom!

This sudden glimpse of that great Dimension, which came to Peter on the wings of Thought, is a revelation. All he knew in that moment was that Jesus was *who he was—"I AM THAT I AM"—* revealed. Everything else about him suddenly made sense. Peter knew no more about Peter than that he stood next to Eternity-made-man. Jesus handed him the "keys" to the Kingdom Gate at that moment. He stood on new ground. This is where the church was raised up.

Peter's second foray into the Kingdom came later, when Jesus left It in his disciples' shaky hands—on shaky ground, we might say. Peter and Company suddenly found that the Ground shook so mightily that they had been swept off their small *premises* (read it both ways!) into that great, wide, plain Truth he had carried within him.

He did not take *it* with him into the grave!

The Kingdom was theirs now, to do with as he had told them, the *way* he had modeled. This time, Peter, James and John, et al., stayed where he had led them. The key was forever passed into their keeping.

The Premise is anything but shaky; it is Rock-solid. The rocks before us are suddenly no longer obstacles, but paving stones and building blocks. We need not shove against them. What we have seen as dire impossibilities, he carves and chisels into new shapes, and fits them into creative juxtaposition with some unseen, undreamt—of Realities only he knows. He gives answer to our great quest and our deepest questions!

He shows us, in some way that will be reality to each, what the land we stand upon looks like to *him*. We are no longer hobbled by our stumbling thoughts.

We walk this Ground in awe and trembling—but the earth no longer trembles beneath. We have come to a safe place—not level, but secure—where there is nothing that cannot be redeemed into a Reasonable shape, and behind our eyes we see new shapes emerge. The images of Love are varied; he alters and reworks as he knows to do, asking us only this:

"*Look!*" The Kingdom is *here* . . . .

∂❧ ∂❧ ∂❧

The geraniums alongside the house are responding to *TenderLovingCare*. What a bright bouquet they make against the peeling paint—a banquet of color, with their pungent red-orange and cerise and shy pink clusters! So much from so little . . . .

This dry place has become my Garden. Even as is its "prototype," the birth-place of our struggling faith, that troubled spot wedged among warring nations, that most unpropitious spot upon the globe—the Holy Land.

Measured by our usual standards of beauty—lushly foliaged hills, towering trees, rushing rivers or dimpled lakes—this is a sere and rubbled land. Like the land of Abraham. But there is a Garden hidden here. It took me much too long to see it, to focus just enough beyond it to catch a different view. It lies unveiled before me now. Perhaps that is the way it always comes to us.

The Garden of Eden—our great *soul-mystery*. It matters little to me whether the Garden of Eden existed as stated, or in God's state of Mind.

Whether we see the Garden as a compelling allegory or our literal birthplace is less crucial to our way of life—indeed, to our "cost of living," our survival, personally and as humanity—than whether we glimpse the spiritual landmarks clearly enough to find our way back to It. We cannot live well beyond the Garden until we have found our way into It.

Incredible Journal or Infallible Allegory, it is essential, bedrock, immutable Truth about the human state of being. It is, in essence, our Home Land, our Createdness, our ordination as spiritual beings. We dare not dispute the *in*tent if we dispute the *con*tent, resigning the mystery to mythology. It is this very erosion that has left us bereft upon our eroded planet.

The Garden calls us home, never ceasing its pull upon our desiccated spirits. All our efforts at recreating it are only *that*. Efforts. We yearn for Eden because we are meant to yearn for it. When we cease yearning, we are either very found or very lost—too content to yearn for more (which is always "less"), or too far removed, too long departed to identify our homelessness.

The Garden is not simply our spiritual grounding, as basic as that fact shall ever be; it is a nagging counter-demand within ourselves for serenity of place and purpose that we openly resist. We are frenetic in our search for what the Garden *is*. We pace and re-pace ourselves, adding insult to the injury of our being. We race *our self* to the finish line and find there are no markings there, no prizes great enough to satisfy.

There are no gardens large enough, real enough, lovely enough to account for or fulfill our Garden-longing. We have been betrayed by our lust for soil and spoil and toil. All of us, in our heart of hearts, know this. Eden is a yearning, a fragrance within which goads us, its pungency haunting our deepest dreams.

Oh, and we have scraped our own earth-garden bare, ripped it up to search its veins. We hold within our dirt-stained hands the severed rhizome, the hidden root of evil.

Where are our forests primeval, and the life they harbored? If Noah were called back to build God an ark today, it would sail half-empty. The earth is *our* ark—this fragile craft that skims the silent sea of space which birthed us. Earth has grown heavy with our woe, with our very being.

When we are at peace with life, with God, we create beauty where before we have left it our destruction. When we are at peace with God, we come to peace with our self. We come into peace with each other, and we offer peace as a gift beyond our own tight concerns. To bring peace to the earth, upon earth, we treat it kindly.

Kindness must include this—that we repay our moral debts. Anything more than life itself is too high a price for tomorrow, for we have given too little and asked too much through all our long delays, our long todays.

Sentencing us to our own destruction would be *just*, but we carry bird and beast and green things on our back. They, their physical reality, are the breath and substance we are made of, the cells that we have been redrawn from. We all ride together on this ark.

When a tree breathes, we exchange life with it, breath for breath, soul for soul. We owe our very life to earth, which shelters us.

The world has been taken apart, piece by piece, and put so poorly back together—like a Chinese puzzle which we lay aside and never solve. Surely we have little propensity toward preservation or custody. Few of us are born, or raised, with the awe, the fervor earth requires of us. We come to it late, many of us, if at all. We remember when things were better, grieve for what we have lost, what *life* has lost, and seldom choose to know how, step by step, act by act, we have misplaced whatever was good.

We must make room in us, among us, for nature, for she has no home beyond us, and we have no other home beneath Heaven. This small planet has shared with us her secrets, her virgin beauty, her wild and delicate and inimitable profusion—shyly, haltingly, as a bride to a groom. And we have sold her—a slave to our varied passions—to the highest bidder.

Let all things which have sound and voice cry out "*Undone!*" Let silent rocks and furies of the wind join in together, grieving over us, calling us to lay aside our hollow splendor for their own.

When we listen to the earth, we hear weeping beyond the human ear. The fog lifts, and we see the truth: that we have made ugliness. The answer for our shame is not to live on in fog, but to find where beauty hides and bring it back.

When we learn to listen well, we will know the secret of its hiding, and the secret of its healing.

❧ ❧ ❧

Today the sky is a dark quilt, wrung incessantly. Here and there its patches have worn thin, exposing heaven . . . So like a metaphor of life, it needs no embroidery!

Stretched on the lumpy sofa with my glass of tea and book at hand, I am free to sleep or read or explore the cloud-breaks for signs of Grace.

Indeed, the rain is the Gift. I am apt to grouse at *Donder und Blitzen,* even though I know it is our great essential—even when I have prayed for it explicitly. How like the fabled Israelites upon the desert! How like the soul of each of us, with our constant tripping over the hard Rock of Grace.

We are not made for storms—but they are made for us. When we are *weathered*—when we *have weathered* enough, well enough to accept and endure the inclemencies around us, our perspective changes. Then the internal climate is altered in some marvelous, gratuitous way. We see both the storm and the Light. If the clouds move, it is not at our bidding but, perhaps, oh, yes I hope so—at our faithful *longing*.

We do not proclaim the climate of our days and ways; we cannot *mandate*. We may, strangely enough, create it, perceive it suddenly or thought after thought. It is in the silent living of it that it may become.

And we? We become "climatized"—all-weather people, moving and living through what befalls, as if the scorching sun upon on our backs struck unheatedly. As if the clouds that loom were meant to shield it, lest we parch from such beneficence.

Like Elijah standing, covered—and open finally.

Open before the sudden face of God.

The week has been languid, the air beautifully scented these past few days. Finally I realized: it must be the peaches. The trees on the far side of the orchard are barely visible, but I zig-zagged my way through the maze of lemons, each hemmed by small, crude ditches, and stood in awe at the edge of peachdom. The fruit is fully ripe now, dangling in heavy clusters, the boughs weighed down as if they groaned in burden.

Never were peaches more succulent than these—or perhaps it is my hunger for such tree-sunned fruit. I couldn't wait a decent walk through the trees to the kitchen sink; my chin dripped with a wash of sticky juice.

The aroma is more Edenic than anything I have memorized in my reveries of nature, more sensuous than any *parfum* that any Eve has daubed behind her nubile ear. But peaches are an apt metaphor for Eden.

God's paradigm—our Garden.

Perhaps *this* was his initial intent: to draw pictures, to become primary (primordial) story-Teller to his clueless kids. To enlighten us, to break open the bedrock Truth of our being, break down our addiction to mental gyrations—the way they twist and turn, slither up and wrap around our thought-life. To break up this blatant cartel of neuroses that prowl among us, blathering their wares.

We are all kindergartners sitting in an arc before him. *"Be still, and know that I am God."*

When we are done with whining, fidgeting—and finally fix our inner eye upon him, we enter the *story* (not *history, but his Story*) of eternal life. At Eden. Always, somehow, at Eden, where everything "story" began and essentially remains. Where anarchy slinked in before us and trapped us, flattered and inspired us. It worked; it often does. The story would never have been writ without our instant, bald complicity.

The Tree of the Knowledge of Good and Evil: we are born of its soil, and the smell of its fruit is sealed in our earthy lungs. And it is more than a peach. Or apple. Or pomegranate, even. A varying aroma.

> *"For God knows that in the day you eat from it your eyes will be opened, and you will be like God, knowing good and evil." When the woman saw that the tree was good for food, and that it was a delight to the eyes, and that the tree was desirable to make one wise, she took from its fruit and ate; and she gave also to her husband with her, and he ate.* (Gen. 3:5-6)

Ergo . . . Eve beneath the dangling fruit. The subsequent dangling of it before Adam. The moment of enlightenment and darkening. The first sensing of subterfuge, of distortion. And ours—we've all been there with them: the sudden grip of craving, too tightly coiled around the soul to argue out of. A do-or-die leap for some perfect composite *mind-body fruit* equal to the heady sin which craved it. And the rationalizations, ah yes!

Yes, we know all too well of evil, and the mental tinkering that begets it and condones it.

Our ancestors had barely (yep, *nakedly* too!) finished gorging on fruit-flesh when who should appear but Papa God? And behold, they suddenly *knew* they were naked. Oops! The first fruit of this new self-consciousness:

a sudden need for less than full disclosure. Maybe the primal fruit was a *fig*, perchance? Its leaves, ah, its leaves were our first disguise!

Okay, the rest of the story is predictable. Their Progenitor kicked them out. *East of Eden* means anywhere outside the Gate, of course. Where lads and lassies have expanded on and "refined" the basics of sin with great ingenuity and avidity (i.e., clever & greedy) ever since.

The emperor's clothes indeed.

Meanwhile, back in is garden, irrefutable suspicion of further woe: the serpent, mission accomplished, undoubtedly shunted down the trunk minus his spent skin, hissing happily, and headed out across the soil of planet earth—following, tracking these new pilgrims . . . and all who came after.

The *story* of humanity was written *there, on* the clay, *from* the clay. The fruit of this unknown genus has flourished. A seed that we are born with? Our lost innocence in itself is no surprise, particularly to YHWH. Surely God knew that there ever would be a bit or more residual mud up our noses.

Late-day shadows stretch across the orchard, heightening every-thing—filtering light and dark with its imperative—every ditch and hump of earth, each irregular hollow. The starkness of dark and light. Each weighted bough from every bifurcated tree: the scent of Grace, the torment of the serpent's forkèd tongue.

These fruit are a promise. Some day Eternity will sweep us along, and when we waken—raised from dust once again in some new Garden of his choosing—we shall see it: the Tree and its fruit. We will *know* it, know its warm aroma, for we have remembered it in all our dreams of Home.

We have never quite forgotten such a taste.

Did you ever raise, or spend time around hatchlings? I watch them avidly here—watch their watching. Tiny skittering balls of goosebumps (chick-bumps?) and sprouting fuzz, they cock their wee heads and eyeball mom and other pace-setters, follow after like little dust balls blowing—and between the raucous cheeps and clucks/squawks, they learn. By genes and imitation they learn. They peck at the earth, testing bugs from gravel. By the time their feathers have fully tucked in, they are quite chicken-wise. They are *patterned*.

Moving along through the history of God's people, we find patterns that predicate both the power and the poverty of our religious history. We see the depth of faithfulness and the spiritual blindness that played out over the ages, from Genesis on through the epistles of Paul.

And we can't avoid the Truth: that the "genome" of sin is mutant and thriving. The *patterning* of the "original sin" (that existential hunger and its offshoots) has replicated incessantly. That old original hunger—for fruit or anything "fruitful" is thriving. It has "gone viral," to put it in today's vernacular. It subtracts in order to multiply. It divides to add. The devious math of Satan. Rampant cruelty and varied thieveries ricochet across the continents. Some brutal, some sophisticated. The severing of heads and severing of hope.

The Old Testament is replete with examples. One seemingly "incidental" story of soul-gluttony becomes for two great religions the most notable, most enduring case in point . . . and portends the endless (thus far) fracture of two genetically related peoples. It shaped and endlessly reshapes the history of Israel, the Palestinians, the Mid-East, and yes, increasingly a *world* in turmoil. *A hunger unassuaged: Genesis 27 and on.*

Esau gave up his birthright for a mess of pottage—a bowl of lentil stew, specifically. (I doubt many of us would admit to the sin of legume-coveting.) But in his hunger frenzy he gave up more than lentils; he lost the "dominant genes" in his heritage. As firstborn, His patriarchal blessing was assured. Until *then*. It went to brother Jacob, who set him up. Jacob the deceiver, the conniver—ah, Jacob the future "Israel," ultimately renamed by the God who knew the beginning and the end of this small-great story.

It was Esau's murderous rage that drove Jacob into the austere life that would transform him. Jacob fled (another long story). Many years and tears later he was humbled enough to head back home and beg forgiveness. Which in itself was a notable step—in a land where men drew blood before asking someone's name. Smiting was the game of choice. The swords have morphed to Uzi's, et al., but the sport continues.

Anyway Jacob, the much-wiser and now-redeemed sneak, snuck back home, fearfully, with a full range of family and possessions . . . and a caravan of livestock as palliative—a *sop*, to put it bluntly—and met his brother. Amazingly, Esau greeted him with equanimity, invited him back, and declined the flocks. It would seem that all was well, finally. But wait! It didn't last.

It rarely does. Jacob's gifts of reconciliation were no match for Esau's hunger. He attached himself to his uncle Ishmael, Abraham's other son, and developed different concepts, married outside the faith, and sought alternative answers to the great Unanswerable.

YHWH had told both Ishmael and Isaac they would father great nations, or the equivalent. And because of the broken tradition—the patriarchal Blessing—Esau and Jacob each became progenitor of a race of Peoples.

> *The groundwork that was laid here has rumbled through the Mid-East for centuries.*

Scant years after the reconciliation, these divergent faith-based social orders, with all their growing list of attendant schisms, were firmly entrenched.

This was chapter one in a long history of fratricide. Two historical people groups, both of whom God promised to multiply exponentially. Two primary persons with a common father, Abraham. Even fervent reconciliation could not stave the brokenness between them that has never ended.

I wonder how, or if, a modern Jacob could model the strength-inherent of *humility* in today's ricocheting discourse and bedlam, and whether Esau would meet him, once again, with tears and open arms. And if, perhaps, it might endure.

What if Jacob and Esau had knelt at an altar together? Where God does his deepest work. Where the cravings and the dark suspicions die in Holy Fire. Where the old ways and means lose their ghastly imperatives.

We all have our lentil-lunges, our moment's demand, the exigencies we yield to. *When we are hungry, we sometimes sell our lives.* When we sell our lives, we often sell our future, and in ways both tangible and intangible, the future of others.

I have known varieties of this lunging for "sustenance." This knife of hunger . . . but have hesitated to equate it with a squalor of the soul. We generally don't—we don't want to. We must; it's part of the human condition. Such hunger goes far beyond a rumbling belly.

Today, *this historic Day*, our "pottages" are killing us rapidly—both personally, and those who suffer from *our* addictions, and from *our* pandering to power—to gain something from the unwitting or impotent, and yes, to gain something empowering from those who are powerful. As a nation, and ubiquitously, as created beings planted upon this small belly of earth and water.

Our bodies bloat; our spirits shrivel. It is a poverty which does not know of, or cannot, *will not* trust in—nay, does not *want* some Provision beyond this moment's promising appeasement. It is a poorness that soothes the dyspeptic attitude or excites our salivating vanity—and starves the cell of us. Such hunger is the *desiccated fruit* of that original ravaging soul poverty—an epidemic beyond the occasional or "low grade fever" of desire. But every small fever degrades the cell of constancy.

True starvation is rampant—the kind that shrivels across Africa, stalks the ghettos of India and South Asia, rides the bony backs of refugees across the Mid-East and ratchets the favelas of South America. Etc., on and on.

Ah, this is personal connivance brought to a vicious fulfillment: The "King's Table" mentality. Imperial gluttony: him that has, gets. A position of authority equates with justifiable (or incontrovertible) rapacity, which is toppled soon or late by others yearning for their own pot of gold. Gluttony is greed, is the ultimate self-indulgence morphed to group indulgence. It is a personal sin and corporate vandalism. It is a blade held to the throat of humanity.

No, mankind cannot live by bread alone. But we can kill for "bread" alone.

It happens all the time, and incrementally. By our voices and choices we feed the hungry, or build our cache. Our national life and often, personal life, is a feeding frenzy. Those who "feed us," and those (the bean counters?) who legislate *them*, who *"feed"* them—are begging the question of intent. The bread of commerce is grown on sterile soil, bathed with toxic brews, and brings ruin to nearly all but their own interests. GMO: GotMyOwn.

Listen . . . we have sold ourselves, our heritage, our destiny, for a bowl of beans. Those who *buy and sell* the souls of humanity for the making of their own "bread" (double entendre here) have little empathy, little cause to share their bounty. Profit steers the ship; poverty is its wake. Such is the legacy of those who sell their souls for a mess of pottage.

And yes, this is "the way the world ends." A long, endless whimper.

The world is consumed by all sorts of hunger. I have sold myself to lesser gods for lesser needs, for lesser reasons than that great, unassuaged hunger which reams us always.

Our cells cry out within us, humanity cries out beyond us. I have turned my back, stoppered my ears, yes, looked away. And always, the weeping of beings of my own kind, those of my own fouled genetics, have followed me, followed me until I shook with the misery of the guilty. No porridge is fine enough to attenuate this indigestion!

Mahatma Gandhi says: *"There are people in the world so hungry, that God cannot appear to them except in the form of bread."*

And he did—for all our poverties, our poor malnourishments.

As recounted in Mark 6, consider Jesus' feeding of 5000 (the men alone being counted). Over and over, he ripped and tore *the meager rations offered by one child*—a pittance of bread and fish that bloomed and spilled from one small basket. *Our meager given over to his abundance.* Watch the Master's fingers digging into the fiber, rupturing it to shreds that unfurl in endless replication!

We are called to do the miraculous; it is his gift to those who know his ways and means. The gift of breaking-making bread, of sustaining others.

And yet . . . we *cannot* live—oh no—on bread alone! None of us.

Jesus fed the bodies *and* the souls of people who came to hear his Words of life—who would not leave despite their grinding bellies. They did not cry out for food. They did not come to eat. He fed them because they lingered so long. They came because their souls were parched and pained.

A gift of bread, or its equivalent, its substitute in the world's vast feeding programs, cannot really solve anything beyond the frantic moment. Famines rage and wane and rage again. Nature and the nature of humanity in collusion—or collision. We must, in some ongoing way, give the needy more than our sacks of grain, our best intent for the day, our way of salvaging their lives this time, this tempest. *This* is not the answer.

We surely know that handouts, precious as they are, will not save the world. They are the moment's best alternative to death. They have never changed anything for long. The sustenance of life must come from those near and far who have some direct control or can change the mandate. And therein lies the nature of this mounting evil.

The world is in spiritual disrepair, is trapped in a mindset that has metastasized and brought ruin across wide swaths of nations. A tide that flows every direction.

The world has grown ever more care-less. Nation after nation has been subverted by incompetent and greed/power-driven rulers, one after another. They murder their people or abandon them to penury and death by proxy.

And we, who are repulsed by such enveloping trauma? We, as a nation, grow inured to the horrors beyond, and beneath, our Lady Liberty's clarion call to the *"homeless, tempest tost"* [sic]. The *Mother of Exiles*, poet Emma Lazarus named her. For over a hundred years she has stood at our entry, stood for America and its heart, for our incomparable spirit of promise. She was our promise. *Was.*

We cannot contain all the tempest-tossed today. The world is reeling with the sum of its broken parts, its broken souls and bodies. With the proliferation of evil. No, not one great pit of dementia like the scourge when that dark "ism" in Europe erupted in hellish fury. Today we watch an "animal fury" sweep across small, unhinged countries that were often cross-stitched together. That are swept by raging tides where once neighbor and neighbor sometimes tilled the land side by side. It is a sick unraveling, a desecration of religion and culture that now explodes where there are no boundaries, no battlegrounds, no rationale beyond the hell that the devil's minions have shaped from the ravages of their dark thoughts.

It is Time to sharpen our plows. It is our difficult privilege to come alongside the hoe'ers and reapers and walk their rows with them. In person or proxy. To go out or send out. To split our loaves and fishes. To pump our water . . . a live metaphor, the grain and the ground of hope.

No less will do. Faith is like that.

❧ 7 ❧

In keeping with its nature

THE ORCHARD IS QUITE dry. When I first came here I scratched little trenches from tree to tree, from basin to basin, and dragged the old, black hose around to fill them. They are eroded now, and clogged with debris. I begin again; the heat is rather unpleasant, but there is a drive in me to do this.

No, I'm not a martyr . . . This is not my vineyard—not in any sense my responsibility. It was never asked of my renter friend, nor of me, and it is only because I need to do it for better reasons than approval that I hack at the dry earth and haul hoses for several hours.

Perhaps it is my gift to nature as much as to the landlady. Bea needs my help less than that of a reliable gardener—quite true! But maybe she needs both. Maybe the trees do too. I know I do—need to be here today doing this thing in the hot sun, even as I wonder if I will shrivel onto the clotted earth at any moment.

It is right to do this. It feels good.

We have largely forgotten sweat equity, fortunate (?) moderns that we are. Our equity in mother earth is earned, I think. If we cannot, will not care for it, invest our time and energy and yes, a bit of our hard-earned money toward its well-being, we have little to complain of, little to expect. Doing small things to help will suffice for those of us in smallish places.

All the usual things are crucial—recycling, conserving, gardening, mulching. But we need to *create*, as well. We need to play god in a way that God himself would do, like planting someone else a garden, watering someone else's tree(s). *Just because.* Without asking for any of the harvest or any thanks. Because, maybe, it starts something and finishes something.

It may put an end to someone's detachment, to alienation, to the kind of despair that rolls over in bed and gives up on whatever creates life beyond mere existence. If nothing more, it puts an end to our own detachment. It starts something pumping inside us that gets to be a "fix," a spiritual/psychological rush. We have begun, in some small way, to change our world and our way of seeing the world. A small price to pay for god-playing.

A very permissible god-playing . . . .

We are custodians. We must be, or we are doomed. I *am* my brother's keeper. It is not my duty to give him an easy way out of responsibility, but to take up my hoe and work alongside when it's clearly needed—under the trees next door, or, by proxy, far from my own front door.

Bea still needs a good gardener, which is hard to find. This plot of land needs more maintenance than I can give. But this present crop of fruit is mine to nurture for these weeks, and it is enough for me that it is full and beautiful and fragrant—ready for someone's pleasure.

My pleasure is in seeing the fullness, and watching a great white goose lift herself joyously, splashing and guzzling and crowing beneath the green boughs.

℈ ℈ ℈

Vesla has gone back inside. She sleeps in her favorite sun-spot on the sideboard, her tail wrapped over her haunches. She has come now into peace with inside and outside.

When we are caged, we want out, of course. Oh, how I know! When we are turned out, we long for the comforts we knew. And when we are able, we pass back and forth unhindered by anything but our hungers. Whatever we yearn for will open a door—although we may not find what we thought we sought. We are spoiled, we moderns, in both senses of the word. We want a lot of whatever we want. We have rotted from the having of it.

I went to Britain some years ago, for a few weeks. I would have settled in and down indefinitely; I was starved for what the picturesque English countryside, and Welsh back roads and cobbled villages, and the timelessness of brooding Edinburgh gave me for those two weeks. Serenity?

Beauty, history, ancient roots, cell memory?

Back home again, I was sated with the experience, and as starved as before I left. I wanted *more*—more travel, more experiences, memories, more inns and pubs and winding roads and hedges and Cockney accents and high teas. I was insatiable. I felt *deprived*, knowing it could be years before *Yorkshire* was once again more than a word to roll on my tongue. I had entered the United Kingdom and fallen in love.

We are not meant to live impoverished lives, but it is not "impoverished" to be denied the Cotswolds, or any other spot, or experience, or life-superfluous thing on earth.

We are impoverished when we cannot live with hope and dignity where we are, and have no recourse for living beyond it.

It is from this that we need rescue, need a timely gift from ourselves and another to begin the trek across the desert. It may be only a few pots of flowers or packets of seeds, or a can of paint or box of paints, a night class at the local high school, or a bowling trophy, or a neighbor with a winning smile and open door.

On my fiftieth birthday, I received such a gift. It was a bleak time, and I would have escaped the formalities, the family "obligatories," if possible. Celebrating was not the prevalent mood—for me or my family. I was pondering the irrelevance of my "day," when the back door slammed open, and in staggered one of my "ad hoc" kids—my daughter's best buddy—laden with balloons (*"Over the Hill,"* of course!), streamers, a bottle of pretty darn good champagne—and the grandest vase of long-stemmed red roses I've ever fingered.

Four dozen of them—and two delicate white ones to complete the count! (They sell by dozens.) The bouquet spread like crimson glory over the table; the aroma was breath-taking.

"Uh, Mom. . ." my almost-daughter said, with a sly grin, *"the white ones are for purity!"* (You know which ones wilted the next day!) I stood there laughing like a goon, tears washing away all traces of malcontent. If *she* believed *I* was worth celebrating, I felt like celebrating. Not my *age*, of course, which was irrelevant, but my *being*. I have never forgotten such a fragrant and flagrant rescue . . .

Each of us needs our equivalent of Grace at a closed-down moment: a walk across the moors of Scotland would be nice; a pot of heather may be the beginning of a finer walk. *"Oh, I'll take the high road . . ."* the old Scotch folksong goes. If we never see Loch Lomond, we are not truly deprived; if we've seen it once, we can rejoice. But if we are locked into a desperation that we alone cannot lift, an *ennui* as vast as life, a pinched place of *being* that compromises that very being, we need "spoiling"—of a sort that is a "hand-up."

Oh, I pray this for you, for each of us—for the receiving and the offering of it!

And I pray something greater—that the spoiledness within us each will stink too awfully to tolerate, that the poverty we hide, within which we hide, will drive us to that higher road that leads Home. It is HomeLand we really yearn for, after all.

Something in us *needs* spoiling . . . for those Reaches of Heaven within our reach.

To cure our rotting.

ɔ❧   ɔ❧   ɔ❧

The orchard is cool with shade and warm with light—that intricate balance which Eternity lays upon its own.

I have been irrigating again. Several weeks have passed since the last "day of hoses," and the leaves are beginning to crisp. The small waterways that I originally scraped out, with a sturdy stick, are still intact and beginning to fill and drain.

They run the length and breadth of the orchard—tree to tree—to catch the overflow of one and another basin.

My main concern was seeing that each tree retained its pool well enough. If the water ran in and out too fast, it would not have time to soak down to deep root level. The surface may be a muddy bog, but it's the deep roots that need the water and the deep soil that *holds* the water.

Indeed, when we have an abundance of trees and a shortage of water, it becomes a delicate matter. As a Californian, this is a daily reality. How well and often do we test the soil beneath the surface? Has it flowed in and out too rapidly, too quickly, left a splash here, a sprinkle there.

And of course you know where I'm heading: What of this need we have for *soaking love?* And, what, indeed is "water" for another?

Our earlobes don't turn crisp when we are dry within. Our hair doesn't fall out—at least not precipitously. Oh, but there are other signs, if we can learn to read them—*if* we want to learn to read them, and know what that learning *is*. There is a gray-ness, a drawn look, veiled eyes; we can read the face, the gestures, or lack of them, for signs of root-thirst. Sometimes I have seen it in my mirror.

The world is full of shallow wells.

Why do we think that a splash, a spritz will do it—that the soul can live on barren necessities? Oh, it cannot! Such watering betrays us all! Our surface "feelers" soak it up quickly and spread out, seeking more, exposing us to droughts too great to stand through.

We die, our taproots die from many shallow splashings!

When I go out of town, others water my myriad plants for me. I have learned a painful lesson: don't assume that people *know* what it is to water thoroughly. Don't assume that people know how to love thoroughly, deeply, vulnerably, unselfishly. Don't assume that *you* fully know this, that I truly do. We probably don't, not *well* yet. I am still learning to test my own root drought, to know what water *is,* to find the variable sources, to measure it out.

The world is awash in shallow relationships, in facile "friendships" that make a lovely splash and go out like a tide. Sometimes our water is brackish or befouled by our contaminating views and viewpoints, our psychic runoff. We are victims and victimizers, all at the same time.

If I cannot offer you something deeper than a cheery hello and glancing peck on the cheek, seeing the grayness in your eyes, the wilt of your shoulders, I have failed to recognize the drought, and will not offer Water. I have shriveled us both.

Several lemons on the trees before me have fallen prematurely upon the crumbled soil beneath. I must watch more carefully for signs of drought before the fruit withers—before the leaves turn crisp. I have learned to recognize the signs; now I must watch for them, know what to each is sufficient Water. And Where the well is.

Have you checked any earlobes lately?

ạ ạ ạ

Early this morning the porch was bathed in mist—a fog that often envelopes the Southern California coastal region in mid-summer. It dissipates to a haze as it moves east, and we are careful to distinguish it from *smog,* which is an ever-present reality. Of course, we tend to call anything fog that isn't brown, in this state of wishful thinking which *is* California.

Fog . . . ah! The pearly haze that softens our harsh realities is sometimes more a gift than an impediment to sight and reason. God, merciful ever, veils the harsh edges of our imperfect life. We are able to see the shape and hue and size of sin—to identify it well enough to avoid collision or to point it out to him, but we could no more withstand the view of our soul through the eye of god than Moses could stand face to face with him without being crisped by Holy fire. *His* haze is not obfuscation, but a wisp of Grace against that glare of Light too great to dwell in.

The mist has burnt off my porch and the hills beyond. What I see before me is an unveiled beauty—spare and dry, but wildly lovely, as only nature unadorned can be.

Above and around it all, hovering like a warning breath, a touch of umber upon the late-morning air. But the earth here is quiet and nature is busy, and the Kingdom Now and Eternal rests lightly, securely, upon us.

I am home.

❧ ❧ ❧

I took an early walk on this Tuesday; hiking is most pleasant in the cool flow of morning. But today the heat was already palpable upon the clumping soil; I could *feel* the orchard pant for relief. We are in a heat wave, but San Diego's dry climate is now becoming humid, due mostly to the great spread of vegetation.

The drought here has been somewhat hard on us, and the restrictions somewhat more unfair to some than others. That happens in any circumstances where restrictions are essential.

But it is not all bad, this deprivation. It forces us to rethink our *place in the sun.*

We are ever unprepared for drought of any kind. We become users simply because we have never known drought. Those born to it take the little they get and make it do more than we can ever conceive.

But we humans have not learned to live *with* nature. We have built pleasure palaces and lush golf courses upon our deserts, have turned our prairies into thirsty gardens, have robbed our rivers and lakes to feed our burgeoning cities—and now we wail against the vicissitudes of nature and inequities of law!

What were/are we thinking of?

This small orchard before me, with its momentary moats and puddles, gives back more than it takes. It does not require more than an occasional drink. But from this "cup of cold water" I pour beneath each tree comes a wealth of fruit *in keeping with its nature, in keeping with nature.* These citrus are survivors here; they ask little, give much. They prove themselves and profit the land. They live at the lip of a well that is used sparingly when there is little to spare. Our civilization used to be much the same.

Indeed, what are we thinking of? What of the vast thousands of acres that gulp gazillions of acre-feet of water and would die day after tomorrow sans the diverted flow? Where do we begin and end our estimation of *need* when faced with the dearth and death of aquifers and lakes far beyond our long, sucking pipes and ditches? The battle between aqueduct and aquifer is nearly over, and we are the losers.

We are, nearly all of us, a profligate people, and our long, virtually unhindered exploitations have taken a tragic toll. The earth is changing rapidly beneath us. For hundreds, *thousands* of years, our brutality to nature had seemingly small impact—small, but accumulative. Now it is exponential. We have lost our race with the future as security, with tomorrow as a certainty.

Not that life itself was ever seen as secure, despite our rapt absorption with securing it. No, rather that we always knew that whatever sporting game we played on the earth's checkered fields, the fields were always *there*, inviolate beyond our violating.

Oh, not so! We stagger, blinded and deafened by our fumes and fantasies and our fatuity, into Tomorrow . . . and find that it is a flower already wilted and dying. This strange winter has set upon us, with its great heat roiling!

It is a hard thing to contemplate what has happened to our earth and to the communities that we live in. We do not want to admit to our own culpability; it is our grief, but not *our doing*. We all want to hide from our effluvia and the assortment of horrors we see around or beyond us.

Ah, but we cannot uproot all our plants and people and shuffle them to a likelier spot. There isn't any. Where can we escape to? Biospheres, planets of another sort, unspoiled? Daydreams? We can, ultimately, only escape from the life styles we have insisted upon at so great a cost.

And history, as we know it? Shall it write of our demise? I pray not! The reality of this dilemma has barely touched our unwilling souls; perhaps it must come slowly, lest we faint from fear. It will cost us dearly to save our future, and politics dictates a bleakness to our survival.

Earth is meant to be our Ark, ever bearing us Homeward. It is becoming our Titanic.

Is there no one at the helm, or on the bridge, who sees the ice floes, or sees the size of them and the course that we have set? Are there no leaders large enough, wise enough, brave enough, to set a new course?

Pogo said it; it has become a painful and pungent cliché: *"We have met the enemy, and he is us."* And so it is, and so it ever has been.

Those among us who *should* do what we *could* do, too often do not. There are other wars, and lesser wars than this, this final battle, to distract us, crises of all shades, and businesses and power plays of our own choosing to absorb us.

May God grant us some vast humility not born of our own proud nature! And may God give us greater souls than those who throw the fraying ropes that hold us! Our leaders and our heroes, alas, often come splashing up from the shallows, where fame and fortune have a greater pull than the tide of history.

Well, it is *my* doing—mine to do! It is *mine* multiplied a hundred million times, and it is mine to stand up to, to pray for, to contemplate with as much rationality as I can gather, and mine to negotiate.

And *yours*—a hundred million multiplied . . . .

Jays are inevitably labeled "raucous." A good cliché!

When I first came up here, they were my instant companions. (Birds are rare in my urban yard; cats proliferate.) It was a delight to watch these birds; they were a joyful noise to me. Now I am feeding them—too sporadically, they inform me.

The jays are squabbling over a small feast of peanuts and sunflower seeds set before them, on a precarious feeder. Feathers fly; it's that intense, when the Johnnie-come-lately's arrive.

"This is my stash! Bug off!"

"Sez who?"

How the pecking order is determined is something I've yet to reckon—whether the same birds always arrive first and have "percher's rights," or if one of a clique of these rascals happens upon this rough feeder during morning rounds. But how they scuffle! What bravado, what bravissimo, what brazen hubris! What wheedling and needling!

What blatant hoarding! They gather nuts frantically (the loose change of jay-dom), and bury them everywhere. And they sit back and wait for the worms to come seeking. Half-buried peanuts dot the property; if roasted nuts grew, we'd have a bumper crop.

Wall Street . . . that's what it reminds me of. Corporate America. Those in the circles of power in the citadels of capitalism that poorly feed us—and fully feed upon us.

It goes on and on—a sometimes blatant, but often hidden, cycle that responds to both need and greed. It generally creates the one from the other.

We lay our small stash, our peanuts, before them. Feathers fly.

Ah, but . . . moving off Wall Street onto Main Street, our sense of reality returns. Life more often moves at a different level that is largely peripheral, tangential, often even immaterial to the corporate machinations of materialism.

Oh, we have our pecking orders—far too many! But we squabble over the small change. We make small changes. These two life processes are large enough to consume us, intricate enough to intrigue us, simple enough to grasp. We can hold them in our talons and work them open.

The scrub jays know their business. We know ours; we aim for a likely tree top, where we can scout and scavenge for whatever seems apt to sustain us, and as much more as we can hold in our beaks and banks. But where the Kingdom—the Peaceable Kingdom—has burst upon us, something shifts. No, not necessarily up or down, or right or left, as we so often do, but a shift from outer to inner. *Way in*—beneath the raucous wants, where need is more than seed, less than the feeders built so gaudily, so tipsily around us.

The Kingdom is a realization that we come to when the hoard is gone, or it tastes suspiciously like the dirt we hid it in, or we know that it wasn't what we really needed anyway. At least not the *way* we got it—that perhaps we reached out too far and missed the deeper need.

It was just peanuts, after all.

> He said: *"Look at the birds of the air; they do not sow or reap or store away in barns, and yet your heavenly Father feeds them. Are you not much more valuable than they? Who of you by worrying can add a single hour to his life?"*

And I say "Yes, Lord! Keep telling us until we *get it*—until we get it right!"

Oh, and would you tell the jays, please.

ॐ ॐ ॐ

Next to me on the porch squats an old white metal chair—the forties' style that is once again popular. This one is an obvious "original."

It is early morning, and overnight an enterprising spider has laced the air between porch post and chair. He curls himself, motionless, in an upper quadrant of his filmy trap, trying to look like a victim, swaying slightly in the breeze.

Now a bee approaches, and the spider unhinges two long legs. Bee detours, heads around the backside, obviously seeing the maze well enough. He heads in on spider who fends him off with a wave or two of leg. They part amicably enough, having sized each other up and decided *seizing* each other was too risky.

There is a tiny, exhausted moth snarled in the spider's sticky filaments. I am tempted to try to free it (which would be difficult without smashing poor moth-lette *and* the web), but this is spider's breakfast—a legitimate catch.

I would not *dare* to compare our machinations and our essential survival skills with the basic life functions of spider-and-beedom. The metaphor explodes into fatuity. But there is a premise here that we have tended to borrow, which has worked well—so well for us, as *guests* of nature, that we have abused it. It has ceased working well. We have become *hosts* of nature, and poor ones indeed.

Call it "trap or track" instinct. *Foraging*, if you will. The birds, bees, and a vast array of flora and fauna have followed this formula to extinction or survival. It is theirs to follow.

Early humanity learned to trap and attack not merely from blind *genus* instinct, but to survive physically, to ensure *today* and build upon its message, unwittingly, for their/our *tomorrow*. They were one giant step beyond the critters in experience of living—an unreachable-unbreachable leap and lunge beyond—in the astonishing capacity that distinguishes us: We are endowed with a *cerebrum*. An immeasurable grant for earthen creatures.

From earth we arose and followed our nose. Followed the scent of green.

But oh, we have over-learned!

In our foraging, we have gone from clubs and spears to spades and plows, and ultimately, from silos to iconic, invisible shopping carts, from the "old oaken bucket" at the lip of the well to the click of a plastic mouse. Simplistic, of course, but a way of saying that over the eons, we have moved past the *dependency* mode into the *dominant* mold. We have built hedgerows and hedge funds, signed deeds and covenants, scraped the land of its covering and dug deep for its lifeblood . . . for our *necessities* and *dependencies*—and, blind as the moles beneath us, tunneled across and beneath the landscape, scraping and scooping and sucking on, ever on.

From guest to host. Earth is seen far less as life-source than personal resource.

When we were still somewhat bumpkins, not far removed from being pests or guests in the Garden ourselves, the foraging instinct was more explainable. The survival of our species didn't, on hindsight, look all that assured. But . . . and a large *but* indeed (No, we weren't all pear-shaped!), the issue was really the same as it is now—not sheer survival, but control. Not survival, but well-being—often at the price of others' comfort or, ultimately, their very lives.

Not to simply survive, but to thrive, at whatever cost.

Read up on Cain. He is our definitive metaphor, if not our literal "father." We are, alas, his children, since he effectively chopped off Abel's lineage. Cain was seduced by the same snake-in-the-grass that struck his mama, and forever hisses and kisses at us:

"If it's not yours, make it yours."

Kill your brother, or Bathsheba's husband, or MacDuff, or the fat guy with a fat wallet heading down the sidewalk, or a few (?) thousand people on the other side of a line you have drawn in the dirt.

The asp whispers, "Tell them: 'This land (or its equivalent) ain't your land; this land is my land—and so is everything I can trap or track upon/ with it!"

We forage each other with our sweet and violent seductions, as we were taught beneath the Tree.

Abel was a hunter, Cain a farmer.

I suspect that Abel had a basic love for all life—and an intuitive gratitude toward God, who makes all things. He had the Shepherd instinct, maybe—the *husbandry* attitude. God was pleased with him, and accepted Abel's sacrifice—and not that of his glowering brother. *This endowment, this God-approval,* brother Cain surely couldn't tolerate, for it diminished him somehow. The Cains of the world are easily offended. His turnips wilted in the heat of his resentment.

I seriously doubt that it was the substance of the *sacrifice*—meat over veggies—that the Lord rejected, but the substance of Cain's *life*. His mindset. His soul-set.

The first-fruits of *our* labor spring forth from modems and sewing machines and teaching manuals. But God knew the fences Cain had put up around his soul, if not his fields. It was his soul that needed sacrificing. Abel had, I would guess, moved past the *me and mine* that ended up tracking and trapping him. The hunter was hunted down. Murder was born here.

We have, then, the *willfulness* of our father Cain.

And Uncle Abel? His genes are still in the pool. Often too recessive to cope with the Cains of the world. They're a hardy lot.

We humans may find, hopefully not too late, that shepherding is more akin to us when our cerebrum sorts it out before him. The cerebral us—than the devious and heavy-handed plots of survival we have taught ourselves so well. Our networks, our webs, have become traps.

Perhaps the Peaceable Kingdom will become what it really is, when our cerebrum sorts it out before him. All of us "lambs and lions" grazing together freely. Maybe those recessive genes will take *dominion* after all.

I have built many a fence in my lifetime, laid a few or more traps, stalked hidden desires. We are most often unaware of our subtle killer instinct; it has become too *decent*, too acceptable, even admirable. Too sophisticated, too profitable. And too unarticulated, sublimated, and, finally, "prevaricated." The real dilemma goes far, far beyond a steak-or-beans mentality. It is a matter of species-survival on both an elemental and intricate level.

How do we live as persons; how do we integrate as societies? Are we—personally, corporately, nationally—predators or peacemakers? Do we see life, society, our neighbor, foreigners, the other sex, our spouse, our God as exploitable?

Ah, there is a richness that does not gather gain.

We *homo sapiens* postulate that we must survive and thrive by taking what is ours (by "right of manipulation") whether it is our necessary pork chops or tofu, our neighbor's wife, our nation's or another nation's land/oil/seeds/water/heritage; a day's wage vs. a thousand-year-old tree; a crack at our "fifteen minutes of fame" at the expense of others' emotional or moral or physical well-being.

Humanity is *religious* in pursuit of what we "need," be it artesian or low-cal beer, the latest designer jeans, an 18th century highboy, an upscale acre or downscaled taxes, instant credit or constant credibility. Or a plethora of "rights."

Tracking and trapping. The list goes on, the beat goes on like a funereal drum roll . . .

What is *ours*? What do we *want*? What do we do to get it? What do we do *with* it when we have made it ours?

Stalk, corner, heap up and hedge?

Tending . . . shepherding?

We squeeze each other into our trapped and trapping minds in order to justify and amplify what is, or could and "should" be ours. Our entitlements, our privileges. What I am wondering here is this: Are some of our rights more *alien* than *inalienable*? Are they really ours, or born of Cain's thrust against his brother's benignity and blessedness? Perhaps the original Garden must be restored *within* us before it finally becomes a reality around and beyond us.

We have pursued our earth in spiderish and waspish ways—stinging and immobilizing, paralyzing whatever might escape our personal and corporate greed. With our giant mandibles we have grasped at earth, at life, chunked it down to manageable size, stuffed it down our bottomless gullets, our expanding craws.

We look out upon the world in turmoil, and see a sticky maze before us. We have trapped each other, somehow. The web is frayed.

❧ ❧ ❧

The landscape here reminds me much of Gethsemane. Doves proclaim peace over the earth, despite the ways of the world; Linda looks quite in place, and the Russian olive and pepper trees, while not precisely "Semitic," lend a certain authenticity against the grove of fruit beyond.

Gethsemane was where he left us, really—or where we left him. The exit and entry point into his Kingdom Come, beyond the bleak litter of our kingdoms.

Yesterday I walked out back, across the hump of this mesa and down the ravine that feeds into the hillocks and small valleys of the ranch. It is so much like the Holy Land. All the old, familiar places that our child-minds painted in great, sweeping strokes become, upon actual viewing, near-miniatures of those mighty scenes we "knew."

The Jordan is no raging river, the mountains only fair-sized hills, with valleys but a howitzer-flame width from crest to crest. The Jordan is too small for all its Implications, even as is Bethlehem—as described by Isaiah.

Israel, whatever its final borders before his Coming, is too small to contain such an Infinity.

But thus it is; thus it always has been. God is good at working in tight places, good at working through a microscope. Earth, his flawless metaphor, is his lovely-ugly Micro*scene*, and Israel, a smallish simile for both Grace and Garden, their flawed remembrance and their tragic absence.

And Sky Mesa . . . the borders of this small, promised (to the builders) land are uncertain only to my unfamiliar eyes. Along its peripheries rusted wires drape over old stumps, around bushes, and become tangled and lost in the undergrowth. But it is all written down, where it counts, where contracts are sealed and sold.

The borders of our lives and nations change and shift, and whatever may be the will or whim of those who enforce or endorse the defining, the final reckoning is his. Of this reckoning, no one knows.

Our wanting of land—our coveting, not merely our need—is an ageless story. The history of our history. Perhaps it is Cain's fierce hunger to possess—this jealousy for the fruitfulness of our brothers' soil and soul.

Our land, or its any and many substitutes, is always too small. We are demeaned by our perceived smallness ranged against the largeness of our neighbor, who may be separated from us in many ways, and resented or, yes, even demonized by his *having* and our *having-not* . . . whatever "it" is. And so the forays, the plottings against his plots; they always have some such groundwork. The history of all our histories indeed! The lusts of the flesh are fleshed-out variants of this primal thrust: *"Be fruitful and multiply."*

We have taken this Biblical injunction very seriously, very personally, conquest after conquest, multiplying field upon field, bed upon bed—spilling seed beyond our own frail walls and fences, and boudoirs.

Our lands and loves pass on into history; we become a part of the soil we never really owned at all. His Kingdom has dimensions far different than our puny reckoning. *"The meek shall inherit the earth,"* he said. Those who *crave* shall "own" their grave, and nothing more beyond it.

This smallish acreage here will soon pass into history, with scarcely a ripple. But not really; It is carved out indelibly within me, and I give it to you freely. Care for it! Care about it! It is our inheritance, and Large enough for us all, and growing larger.

The Kingdom as mustard seed.

ﻉ﮳ ﻉ﮳ ﻉ﮳

❦ 8 ❦

The shape and outlines

THE EARTH IS GOD'S altar. It has been called his footstool, but it is *our* dirty feet upon it, not his. So altar it is, is meant to be. The theology of this is less important to me than the spiritual/physical reality. If this is indeed his altar, it is a holy place, a sacred gathering of stones piled and heaped in no random way. It is built to specifications inherent to altar-building in his universes.

That this altar we inhabit is circular, rather than an elevated rectangle is brilliant—rather like a stage-in-the round, where the actors may be seen and perhaps engaged with from any point of view, any angle. The whole of Heaven is engaged, to be sure, weeping and laughing often, and sometimes, too seldom, I fear, cheering.

Shakespeare famously described our world as a stage, and we as "players." Ah, yes! We are all ingénues, trying out for whatever part we fancy in life, or whatever role seems left to us. The part may not suit us, as we shall find One Day, when the Curtain rolls aside. Some are chosen by our choosing "the better part," like Lazarus' intuitive sister, Mary, who chose/received a starring role. Some are "chosen" because there's no visible, viable choice. May they play it with dignity, or humor, or unmitigated hope.

And so our altar has become a stage. A shift of metaphor—and yet *not so*, for an altar is a staging of that great drama of Sacrifice, which we are called to stage and re-stage each day of life. (The hardest of roles to learn well!)

The altar is elevated, raised to a level higher than our dirt-filled eyes, above the sometimes thankless toil that holds us here as "stagehands." We are invited to look up at this long Passion Play, to raise it upon the altar of our intuition, lift life high before him, beyond the despoiling of our dirty feet.

We have often trampled upon his altar, for all these millennia—treating earth as our private possession, our casual toy, our *soil-servant*. We ask much and more of it, to make much and more of ourselves. *As individuals, as peoples.*

Now we begin to see the Truth—that we have caused death and destruction when Life was the great Cause, the real drama.

The altar has crumbled badly, and we search about clumsily through our box of tools, desperate for new tools—to dig deeper, reach further.

Christ yielded his life *for* us, gives Life *to* us. his passion for his earth-brethren has not waned. We know *about* it. But few *know* it, really live it, rehearse it, applaud it, sitting in the front row with Lazarus's sister Mary.

The Drama of his death and resurrection has never ceased playing out before us, center stage. The Play goes on, will ever go on until the End, and we hold our breath and wonder at the final scene.

It is Christ, not us, who will arise and raise the dead.

One day, less far than perhaps we guess, he will step on stage again, without the old familiar props we know so well (from the "bathrobe dramas" in the church hall). We shall all see him, and know him, and the cry shall ring out, rise, with a great crescendo of applause, over the altar of earth:

"*Author . . . Author!*"

❧ ❧ ❧

Afternoon shadows stretch from tree to tree, and I am sitting beneath their shelter. The radio thrums with the passion of Rachmaninov; my feet waggle automatically to my favorite passages.

Bliss . . . The concerto soars to its conclusion.

And then the news intrudes. From the sublime to the ridiculous? No, no—not ridiculous. *Vicious.* More and ever more, death is becoming a mordant and morbid exposition, an endless parade of phantasmagoria. From every quarter of the globe comes word of new atrocity, new frenzies of violence and hatred. From far-away, unpronounceable places, from our comfortable suburbs and, of course, at the bleakest cores of our communities, where despair so often spreads on a turbulent tide.

Anger spews from mouth to mouth, group to group to city to nation—and bursts like wildfire from the barrels of guns. Such pervasive violence, such undeclared, personal or group vendettas were virtually unheard of some decades ago, beyond the nation's battlefields—and not or never on such a scale as this.

We humans are a haunted race . . . .

But it has always been there, been *here*. Within us all. Christ said as much when he walked alongside us. He saw through the thin veneer of our inherent goodness, our presumed civility—saw how humanity behaves when the heat is turned up, when the pressure is turned on, when the "spigot" is turned off.

It *is*, now, "the best of times—the worst of times."

In a world of technological miracles and legislated manners, we still look in the mirror and see, shadowed as they are, the savages who dwell within us.

We die for each other; we lay down our lives for each other—when we believe in Life.

We kill each other—when our souls have died, when we are afraid of death.

We do either, daily, in small ways, with a quick, instinctive impetus that either creates or destroys. All that we carry, all we have nurtured within us will tell its tale.

Violence. The children . . .

The faces of children are the hardest part. We want to gather up the little ones—the innocents, the real victims—gather them in our arms, shelter them, kiss their cheeks, rock them until the fear leaves their eyes.

Oh, the children! When, or if they grow up, they may well kill each other.

Jeremiah wept over Jerusalem long before Christ came to invade it with his wash of tears:

> "'Peace, peace,' they say, when there is no peace. Are they ashamed of their loathsome conduct? No, they have no shame at all; they do not even know how to blush. So they will fall among the fallen; they will be brought down when I punish them," says the Lord.
>
> He went on talking to Jeremiah, to us: "Stand at the crossroads and look; ask for the ancient paths, ask where the good way is, and walk in it, and you will find rest for your souls."

Only beneath his cool shadow do we find surcease from our heated hearts and ways. Here upon this small and Spartan ranch there is a peace that can only be called *luxury*. Often during the days I remind myself of this privilege. And when the guilt for being here, for *having* this, engulfs me—and it sometimes does, when so many have so little—I walk out upon the meadow, where I can see for a great distance. It helps. I stand silent, overwhelmed with the pain I see, yearning over life upon this heated earth, willing such a peace as *this* upon the world.

Willing a Sabbath rest upon the world.

"Peace, peace . . . ." It will not come easily, such a Sabbath.

Above me the branches fidget lightly; their shadows dance easily, back and forth, across my outstretched legs. On the radio, the concerto rises and falls in its lessening and strengthening, like a turbulence of thunder . . .

Like a fervent storm come down upon the airwaves.

Like a great and lovely storm, a cleansing.

Walking across a stubbly meadow at the edge of a sudden arroyo, I brush aside, and against, all his leafy evidences. The scents and sights and sounds of Creation engulf me.

"The earth is the Lord's . . . ."

And *today* the earth *is* the Lord's, renewed and purged for the moment, for this small moment! Genuflect! The sky is a wonder—a great belly, a blue cirque that thrums with all the sounds of Creation. It is a wash of cerulean wonder I had almost forgotten in the grime of this befumed environment. Some kindly zephyr has blown through with a trace of rain, a taste of rain! "Mercy-drops."

The week has not been pleasant; the city smog had built up beyond its usual dull haze, and spread beyond the usual limits. But *today* . . . it is as if a hollow wind had come through and sucked up all the drab effluence, filling itself full of what we fill the air with.

Where does it go, this tawdry plague of chemicals? Someone else is breathing the exhaust from my car. I breathe theirs each day—residue from Los Angeles and Tijuana and far beyond. And we are heading into exhaustion . . . .

Earth is becoming a smoke stack. If we do not rally, it shall finally be our crematorium. I breathe my way cautiously through each day, through our varied fumes, jaws clenched hard against the trembling of my chin.

For I am afraid, afraid of what I know of us, afraid we will not wake up from the soothing hypnosis of our many mantras. Afraid we will accept the choke within our lungs as passively as we do the choking of our souls. Here in parts of the Southwest, we sometimes see no more than the shape and outlines of the distant hills we live by, for all the exhaust and the exhaustion that engulf us. Is hope no more than a fuzzy outline of what was carved out with such sensitive Precision once-upon-an-eon ago?

Our grip upon the earth, upon life, has been forever tenuous. Never more so than now, with so many of us grasping. So much has slipped through our fingers—our earth and sky and waters, as once we knew them, our sense of place within an ordered world, an enduring world. Our sense of security within order. It is as if the world revolves—with us clinging hazardously upon some failing axis—rolling, tumbling, fighting gravity and the pull of those gravities which add up daily.

I think our tenancy here inevitably must hinge upon our knowing, upon our grasping this: *The world is failing around and beneath us. There is no one else but us to pick up after us, to pick up the pieces. God gave us full custody. We are not listening!*

A ferocious confidence has accompanied civilization's advances and refinements. The "truths self-evident" that long sustained society were already unraveling beneath our plucking ways before the evidence became uncontroverted. Like the flora and fauna around us, like the melting of the earth's poles, our verities disappear in a haze of smog and psychobabble, leaving only a semblance to remember, to hold on to.

And now our hands are too often empty of content, full of our discontent. The rain forests smolder; civilizations burn with raging brutality; our planet dries or drowns steadily, increasingly . . . the losses are catalogued endlessly. At a crisis stage in our history, as we have staggered through a new millennium, we cannot ignore the pending disaster.

To do so *is* the disaster.

What must we do, what must we wrestle with, and where do we come to rest? Where do we come, *to rest?* What must *I* do? *I must do something.* Not "any something"—not a frantic search for a solution, not joining a cause to mend the cause of *this dissolution, that* desolation. No, that comes second. It's too big for that . . .

Today invites me to ask for more—for something greater. I choose it. The sound of the universe, the smell of this *new* air compels me to this time of wrestling, to find a rest I have longed for . . . and long resisted. It is as if the smog has invaded my spirit. I sense that I am here, at this ranch, to make peace with both the smudge of my soul and the turning and faltering of this smudged earth. Hope. I, *we* need *hope.*

Is there a hope that is more than an empty postulation?

I believe in it. I must . . . for today the sky reveals it—revels in it.

The clarity of this moment is like a door swung open—like an invitation. Ah, vision! I can see now, again, what I had nearly forgotten: the Kingdom of God as a pledge, a surety. Already the signs are visible. The Kingdom is very near us indeed.

Something *live* is thrusting up, beneath the surface of our woe. It is not strong enough yet to call it movement, or a force, only *a tendency*. But under all the mulch of grief, anger, fear, hubris, malaise, denial, greed, there emerges—here, there, everywhere, in an unlikely ubiquity born of necessity and poverty and, yes, even of vision—new shoots of Grace and its flowering: *sustenance.*

Sustained and sustaining intervention. It is a welling-up and a flowing forth.

Oh, this is where it begins; this is how hope comes! This is how God comes to us. The Kingdom of God is under constant assault. Matthew says it is "taken by force." It is diminished by those capturing and doing spiritual violence to the good within and around us. It is this supernatural-and-all-too-natural blindness, bitterness, brazenness which captures us humans, and violates our vision of ourselves . . . and each other. The only power that can come against such ruination is inherent Goodness.

Goodness? It is part of a counter-plot that sets God's people upon a new plane, a higher ground with unlimited Vision. If we have tasted goodness, as defined by Jesus—fed upon it, assuaged our endless thirst with Living Water, we know: we know the battle plan to gain back God's earth from this growing atrophy. To keep it from drowning in its own tears.

We know all that matters. Goodness: systemic kindness.

"Random acts of kindness" are not random at all, but a new Nature gathered to the heart and poured out. Shrugging off apathy. Walking barefoot through the fire of fear, calloused only to the searing of our own proud flesh.

Doing unreasonable sacrifice. Sacrifice is a plow.

God hears the rumble and clatter of our protests; he waits for us to stop our lamentations, and to turn, and turn again. It is his Time set before us. When we ask for our tools, our "ploughshares," I know they will be set before us, each one to the shape of our soft and clumsy hands, to the shaping of our own germinant abilities. The Kingdom comes to us by the moment, in the movement. Hand to hand to hand.

I believe that Life will be given back to us there, where the prayer greets the plow. I believe that when our focus shifts from self-placation to a hearty Replication, something small and fierce and wonderful, and incremental, begins and begins and begins. This is surely his Kingdom!

When, one by one, by many thousands, by millions, we pick up our pledge cards to life and write down what it is we must do, *are Given to do*, and we *do* it—small unto largely—*it is done*. We will have expelled the enemy and invaded the kingdom of despair!

Hope is more than a promise. Hope leans on a shovel. It is extruded from the sweat of those who dig another man's foundation. We may yet reclaim the desert we have made of earth and of our souls.

Somewhere, over the rainbow, the sky is still beautiful.

Genuflect . . . .

ھ ھ ھ

It was not much past dawn when I slipped out the door and faced the great iron gate out back. In the slant of first light it resembled somewhat the "gates of hell"—heavy and formidable. Ah, but beyond lay Paradise! In lieu of unlocking and unwinding the heavy chain and shoving against its grudging "joints," I climbed over the old monster. I always do—depositing whatever baggage I tote over on the other side.

Today I toted only a weight of weariness. The "world was too much with me."

I am not an up-with-the-roosters person. I felt quite uneasy leaving my comfort zone so early—regardless of the discomfort that routed me. Testing my legs and blood sugar and ignoring the grind of an empty belly seemed like a bad answer to a bad question. Or quest. The gnaw of guts was only a mimic of the churn of thought that woke me.

But I was brought up short by the exclamatory. Earth-life stretched around me, hummed and chirped, exhaled its varied aromatic breaths, each its trace of *pneuma*. The land was filled with freshness. I breathed vastly, enfolded in the small celebration before me.

The early light is a peach-hued wash against the umber earth. An incredible palette! This is the morning's work within me, this facing toward the light. Too often I see the world darkly, see only the umber without the wash of ruddy gold. There are times, even in this become-sacred place, when melancholy overwhelms any sense of the mystery of nature, a denial of the spare and eloquent mastery of God. Scales creep over the spiritual retina I peer through—opaque, filmy, all the drab distortions that we know.

Probably it is much like the blindness that the Lord peeled away from Saul-become-Paul. I recognize this more often now, this clumsy and yes, futile shield—my fascia, a veneer against the callousness before me . . . and within me.

And against grief. There is a sorrow, a *Weltschmertz*, weeping up through me, a deeper grief than I can carry. Either to live without grieving or grieve without recourse bequeaths fatalism, begets tragedy. It is a betrayal of the faith we first consent to.

It is balance I need, and a robust vision. I am just beginning to face *this* truth: *I must neither fear the darkness, nor accept it, nor shrug it off. I cannot fight the battle for earth-life unless I have fought the battle for my vision.*

As a frail and sometimes fatuous human being, I balk at death's increasingly harsh preliminaries—at the way it visits us at every turn, the ways it comes ripping through humanity, Grim Reaper that it is. It is my own creeping entropy I battle, and lose within the entropy of a world I gather up and mourn. It is attending a funeral endlessly repeated, a cortege of the helpless and the homeless.

And the heartless. That eternal death . . .

Life today is often seen as something of a wedge between two vast intangibles—our very entity caught in a grind between the beginning and end, those eternal mysteries of *being*. Nature denies such hopelessness. Every new morning, new spring, each rebirth from fire or flood or wind proclaims life's frailty and strength, unwraps the earth from its grave-cloth. Celebrates its endurance, its stubborn resurrection.

There are no funerals in Heaven. As a believer in the sacred History of faith, I accept death. It is the [often] hard shell we must break through to begin our flight into Life. It is moving from chrysalis to Chrisom, perhaps. Our ultimate birth.

To Christos. Truth is an upward spiral.

I despair of the despair that we wear so often as an arm band, the existential angst we endlessly proclaim, which leaves no room in the soul for resurgence, for resilience, for *hope*. And now I see that *I* also have done this! What a vast, a blind betrayal!

Those who cannot celebrate life destroy it—destroy others, who in turn destroy.

What they cannot celebrate, they desecrate.

And living must be, the soul insists, a celebration. *To exult is to exalt.* To proclaim the tender truth and rollicking affirmation of faith is to live beyond mere enduring. It unleashes the neurons that fire the thoughts that fuel the muscles that raise us up from indolence.

Such is the House that God built. Existential pleasure must bring a recognition, a small ecstasy of awareness—*I am alive, alive, ohhh*! And I am not a cockle, not a mussel. Living is surely meant to be an endless orbit of *meaning-full*, an upward cycle that siphons finally into that slender Passage which is not, oh no, a dark hole.

Entropy is a ravage only of the temporal and temporary and intemperate.

And so, *today*, I lay down this weight of timeless grief against the splendor of *this* day, against the altar of *these* rocks, this gravel I stand upon, with the incense of this morning still awaft like a certain holiness within my breathing.

I celebrate *being*. Despite the daily horrors, despite the anguish surging, despite the fire of grief that still looms, ever creeping, like the ghastly glow of holocaust beyond us. I celebrate because I must; because we must, because God hears and surely answers . . . or this maelstrom will consume us; it will be a prophecy fulfilled.

I celebrate what it is to be truly human, what it means to share the earth together, what it has been to us as home away from Home, what it must become within us and among us, and beyond us, for our children. What we must become, within us and among us and beyond us.

Celebrants. I celebrate the very fact of life, of seeing these shaggy carpets of green-and-ochre and the wild-painted skies that cover me, of hearing the chirrup and buzz and flutter of small life, of knowing earth-born labor and labors borne of the heart.

I celebrate the being of you who cross my path this day in thought or step, who share this swath of earth or one dissimilar, who grieve for its poverty and share its richness with me. Who enrich *my* poverty.

I thank God for my life, for giving breath to my halting aspirations. For *your* life and finest hopes. For his breath upon you, within you.

I thank you, oh God, who redeems me from myself in this small celebration! Who calls me to Rest. Who gives me today geraniums, and a new, eager flow of thought. For doughty ferns in pots, and doughty friends who force my rusty gates; for violet sage and stippled rocks to catch my eye, to catch my breath, my soul.

I praise the God who sprawls his name, and the signature of his Son, his *Chronica Christos*, across the bursting universe and weaves it deep within the spiral of our genes.

> Who walks the waves still, always . . . stilling them,
> forever stilling them.
>
> *Truly the gates of hell shall not prevail.*

૱ ૱ ૱

Over this long-short season I have narrowed down. There is less of me to scatter abroad, and I have found more reasons to live now than ever before. To hear the doves' discussions and the crows' caterwauling is worth rising out of bed, sluggard that I am at dawn. Hearing nature's news is a critical matter—storing up their constant reassurances against the harsh insanities, and inanities, that we call "news." There is nothing *new* about either, other than their immediacy.

No, these things are not pleasant enough to want to get out of bed for in the morning. Listen to the doves, whose "word" has never changed. The certainty of God is found neither in our breaking *of*, nor blind and blinding adherence *to*, traditions and taboos.

We have grown weary of our whoredoms. We have slept with the enemy, and every casual stranger, too many times to be titillated any longer. We have lost our reserve and all our reservations, and nothing seeps back into the fissured, rock-lined wells we draw from. The reservoir is dry.

We have done it again, oh yet again—coasted down history's long incline of expediency and brash exposure. Here we huddle, fig leaves askew, yearning for good old days and a covering we never really knew we had.

It's our collective memory we carry, imprinted back behind the verminous clutter behind our eyes. We "remember" what our cells proclaim—what our genes once knew in deeper ways.

Certainties existed, as uncertain as they sometimes proved to be, as fretful as we were with them. When? It doesn't matter; we knew of them, and yearn for something as unwavering, as resolute somewhere beneath our modern proclamations, behind our screech for freedoms. Perhaps our tendentiousness, and casual wallowing in smut, and the adamant dehorning of our sacred cows is less a need to break down our strictures than *a symptom of our brokenness*. Perhaps our cows these days are only clones of something real, of an essential.

Our appetites for flagrant sex (of all "genres") and precocious "demythologizing" and mindless hedonism, for the right to be vastly wrong, may be less a seeking after "freedom of expression" than a seeking to express our lostness—as if to fling it on the page or screen, calling it art, or truth—or inalienable rights, codifying it on our equivalent of parchment—will make it all somehow acceptable and noble, a shared experience that we must tabloid. A license for the licentious.

No, it's not news, our unraveling. Our primal screams for rights betray our great, heartbroken shriek for *certainty*. Certainty means, today, I can always count on *yes*; nobody will ever rob me of the *yes* I need. We are demanded to say only *yes* to each other!

And so we truly speak "with forked tongue," splitting our *infinities,* garbling and distorting down to shibboleths all that we ever knew that checked our nature. *No* is not correct; it stirs up all the old ghosts of stricture and deprivation and bigotry that we wish were laid to rest. It isn't "fair" because it denies us what we want!

Never have I heard it said that God is fair. Fair is what *we* want. Oh, we want it slanted to *our meaning*, if you will—leaning just a bit to our presumptions, our persuasions, tilted slightly to our "objectivity." God's *no*'s are too big, too forbidding to risk lightly.

I cannot imagine "fair" on the lips of Jesus, as he weighed the souls before him, measuring them against that Silence which he, he alone, could hear.

Fair? Oh, no; God is not fair with us! The thief steals Heaven, squirming in agony on his cross-beam; the cripple leaps forth from his long whine beside the waters, complaining against man and the angels; the whore picks her way through the litter of stones, and walks off free.

Scott free! Well, almost. *"Go . . . and sin no more."*

We should do so well, we well-doers, we jot-and-tittlers.

Not fair? No, the cross is not *fair* at all . . . .

We dance with our ghosts in a most macabre waltz. Oompahpah—two-step, side-step, back-step, leap ahead . . . .

No no no! But only God can say *yes* and *no* to us in the same Breath. We don't know this, really—don't know what his *yes/no* means. It is too frightening to consider one more denial, the Ultimate denial, when my whole being is tied to preservation *of* my being.

God is bigger than freedom and rights and equality. Without knowing this Certainty, we will never know any of the above. We will simply go on struggling blindly against each other, in-the-name-of-whatever, and miss the great Reality.

But oh, paradox was never easy. Like life . . . .

It's the difference between lower and deeper.

When that great, eternal *no* comes thundering down the causeway of his Kingdom, it leaves a deep wake of Love. *Wake*—a wave, a death watch. Take your choice. Something dark within us drowns, goes under, finally. *No* becomes an act of mercy which sweeps us from the flotsam we have plunged through. Like the salt in the sea which buoys and stings, his *yes/no* sustains our weary soul. We are, then, free to explore a new concept:

Certainty. At last!

Here, in this outpost, this sanctum of our fine, rough verities, the birds proclaim all the news that's fit to print; the birds sing *yes* to all we have ever really wanted.

Oh, Jubilate!

ॐ ॐ ॐ

I have been hiking again along the rutted roads (if you can call them roads) which dip and climb over this terrain. This is nature at its most elemental, unadorned, no flourishes or flourishing. I like it for this, for the realness, for its struggle to survive, its ordinariness. We are prone to artifice, to creating substitutes to nature where it offends us. It has been costly. It has robbed us spiritually of the durability that was once ours as a people.

But the *Kingdom* of God suffers not, not at our hands. We cannot rob God of the eternal. This Kingdom of his is no LaLa Land, no Over-the-Rainbow. We cannot improve upon it, cannot ravish it, can do no more than yearn for its revealing.

This is where *Life* and *living* meet.

This is the answer to a California deep in drought, or a nation deep in debt, or a Mid-East mired deeply and viciously in fratricide. This, the fulfillment of that long, sad *Via Dolorosa*—the endless trail of sufferers who create havoc by their very being. This Kingdom is their HomeLand.

Within *Its* provinces the rules change, the "battle" changes, the whole view of life is unalterably altered. The world is made more whole in some small aspect *now*, in one small corner or concept for tomorrow, for the greatest of reasons:

His yearning over it, and our yearning to yearn with him.

God's "foolishness," his wisdom, is a Secret well-guarded; a secret Well, guarded. When we, like Peter, have received that revelation which says *it is*, because *I AM*, we will find it. We live in the Kingdom by invitation. The invitation is ubiquitous. No exclusions. Jesus dined with thieves and died with them.

We are all thieves. We are all invited.

The Kingdom of Heaven is a height worth climbing, a road worth struggling upon, a breadth of vision beyond our poor myopia. It is all Rest and Movement—letting go and adding on, reaching down, moving up, into summaries of Life he opens before us.

He says "*Listen!*" and we hear the world's anguish, and we see its fragile beauty. We hear each other's sorrow and see each other's fragile beauty beneath the ugliness. I hear *your* great, silent cry, and carry your brokenness, your brittleness into his presence, where he proclaims your waiting beauty.

Climb into his Rest with me.

ક ક ક

This morning, as I stood by the dining room table, I was caught by a tiny shadow in the periphery of my vision. I looked out the door. On the porch, not six inches from the doorsill, a small gray bird—a titmouse, I am sure—perched on the rim of a planter. She was peering down behind it, head cocked intently.

I was, of course, surprised: a bird coming so near her human enemies, and particularly the cat, which had no doubt stalked her before and would again.

Birdie disappeared behind the planter, and I waited. Suddenly she was up again, gripping the hard black plastic with her flexing feet, as if doing a little dance upon it. Billowing from her beak was a great tuft of . . . *cat fur!*

I could only gape in wonder as birdie adjusted her "find," rolling it back and forth in her beak, pushing it against the edge beneath her, catching up the stray wisps that drifted. She missed not a hair cast off the cat's body. Each one was "counted." Each one *counted.*

Off she flew, with her light and rather awkward load. Her strange and wonderful gift! Surely it reeked of her enemy, the predator which she had, from hatchlette on, avoided with all caution.

From the hair of her enemy she weaves her nest. With a bit of soft fluff from the underbelly of her torturer, she will cradle her eggs and coddle her own hatchlings. They will grow with the smell of *cat* in their lungs.

Cat fur? Inviting her enemy into her "home"? Would her offspring not grow up heedless, careless, having been nurtured in the sweet smell of their enemy? Wouldn't the smell *cat* mean life rather than death?

I thought about it awhile. I'm still thinking of it . . . the imprinting of wild life, and what this new observation means to me. What I could learn about my enemy, *my* predator.

"Know your enemy," he said. The roaring lion—a great tabby or Truth distorted. How can a bird know a non-roaring lion that stalks in silence? By the time it is convinced of malevolence, it is caught on the prongs of a vicious mouth.

We grow up with the scent of malevolence, the aura of life's blasphemies surrounding us, perhaps *enveloping* us in soft, fuzzy thinking. How do we know, how can we learn what every bird knows—*that the hair is not the whole*? Our imprinting must include, somehow, the smell of our soul's enemy, of our enemy's soul . . . or we will never know him.

He prepareth a nest before me, a present of mine enemy.

 махмахмах

There are predators here. A chain of predators, of course, each feeding upon something smaller.

Last night at dusk, Vesla chose to go out. I consented without a second thought. An hour later, my mind absorbed by other matters, I was arrested by a frantic screeching at the back door. It intensified to unearthly proportions as I fumbled frantically with the lock. When I flung the door open, I heard a scuffling; when I finally found the light switch (ah, how slow we are in other folk's houses!) I saw a dark shape disappear around the corner. It was larger than a cat . . . larger than a breadbox. Several small tufts of fur drifted across the cement floor. I was trembling by then, and could only assume the worst. The sudden silence hung like a malediction; I had visions of Vesla's plump body being dragged into the brush. I began to grieve.

The flashlight was in the bedroom, and I wove my unsteady way back there, literally bouncing off furniture. Outside, there were only the familiar night sounds and a million stars. I ran from the back to the front porch, flipped the switch, and flooded the yard with light.

No dark shape hunkered over a small, prone body. I called the kitty. Suddenly, from a far height in the pepper tree, a small shadow moved and crept down a fork of trunk, belly to the bark. Vesla's frightened eyes reflected in the flashlight glow. She slithered into the house and under the dining table, where she began an anxious self-examination and grooming. She wouldn't let me touch for her for some time—until she had checked each part of herself for damage.

Vesla escaped with her life. Neither of us will forget this warning, I am sure. "*Outside*" is not safe after dark—nor even in daylight, beyond the paths and open spaces.

There are predators here, among us. A chain of them, feeding upon the human race.

We humans, with our predatory ways, destroy most casually. It is a complex power-play, this world and all its powers, the unseen "world" and all its principalities. The overlap is far beyond our recognition or understanding (more's the pity!), and the Evil that breeds our evil does not see fit to enlighten us as to its nature—his nature.

I never believed in Satan until I met him. I grew up in a college environment, a "faculty brat." *Fundamentalism* was a dirty word. Today it is even more so . . . under the assumption that anyone who accepts Original Sin as a doctrine is hopelessly out of tune with real life—is an anachronism in this enlightened world.

Alas! Just as Satan's best argument is his non-existence, so his second ringer is the utter fabling of our spiritual history. Hear me out:

Evil is. It's name, as Jesus spoke it, is Satan. I learned that decisively, many years ago, in an experience I will not share here. (Our spiritual landmarks are not always clear to others.) But a thought did occur to me one day, prior to That Day of Awakening. I was thinking of the remote possibility that there was a, harumpf, ahem, *devil*. In my mind, a question immediately presented, with great simplicity: "*Is Good personified?*" "Of course," I thought. One piercing word followed: "*Howso?*" "In Christ." "*Thesis, antithesis.*" Only these two words, thumping into my consciousness, shifting everything into their proper polarities.

Nothing more than that, but the adamant simplicity of those words startled me.

Over the centuries, our sages have described so passionately, often poorly, this broken world to us (who understand even more poorly!). I am aware that there are certain premises, or perhaps more accurately, "natural laws," that shape or affect human thought and response. In my shamelessly simplistic mindset, I will call this premise the Law of Opposites. It keeps all things together, keeps entropy from destroying us, keeps us from falling off this rock . . . and, moving from nature to human nature, keeps evil in its/his place. For evil is an imbued force, a power, a hammer raised against God. And God keeps *us*—by the "gravity" of our attraction to him, the pull of his great love—keeps us on his Rock, which stands firm in the sludge of Satan's meddling.

In the Eternal kingdom, there is no *synthesis* of good and evil. No *antithesis*. Here, on our own rutted rock, in a world of constantly shifting polarities, we are torn by our own personal tugs and shoves. It will continue until his coming.

Oh yes, the predators are here among us! By their bitter fruits we know them. By the blighted fruit of our thoughts, we are invaded and deceived and taught dark hungers we were never required to know. Each of us has tasted the succulent fruit of pride dangled before us. We have all thirsted for the sweet and heady brew of power, of addicting lusts, or have fed our grinding bellies on the harsh bread of despair.

He comes, this dark angel of light, he comes as lover, as monster, but he comes to each of us—in vague, subliminal glimpses that we scarcely see. He comes again, again, until our eyes are all blinded and we are all contorted of soul. In whatever guise, he feeds upon us all—in small nibbles, in ravenous chunks. By intricate ploys and blatant deployments he divides and conquers and devours.

Yes, there are predators out there, beyond us, among us, within us. Turn on the Light; you will see a dark shape scurry off to some bleak region we have all passed through or dwelt in.

The Kingdom comes to us there, a warm Reflection in our frightened eyes.

≥ ≥ ≥

Annie is beating her wings nearby, defending her turf against a stray pigeon. The pigeon flees, probably for the umpteen-hundredth time. Annie mutters to herself like a disgruntled housewife chasing rogue boys, and ambles off to check the other parcels of her inheritance. What's hers is hers. There's nothing silly about a goose!

She looks a little like some of his servants, as we stalk the halls and corridors . . . *and* consider the budgets and rosters of our Inheritance. The church has grown defensive. It is under attack, increasingly, as the world grows more fragmented, more polarized. But it is more than *that*.

The church has been too long without the fullness of his Power. Too long with-*out* the sanctuary/fortress rather than *within* it. We have moved beyond its protective scaffolding.

We have been building our own great complexes, our lexicons of Grace, our images and imagery—adding outbuilding after outbuilding, proclaiming his name over them. And, as of old, he has often disappeared quietly into the wilderness, seeking his Father's counsel. The people have scattered, seeking him elsewhere or disbelieving, not finding him *here* where we have announced his presence. They have gone to parks and beaches, to Disneyland, to Magic Mountain . . . and yes, to other spiritual realms that hold more promise of fulfillment.

"*What you see is what you get.*" No, often not. We bring what we need—or want (which is not always our real need)—into our seeing, and either settle for something less, a wary compromise, or perhaps something more—something different, or *promising* (which is not always our real "more"). Or we walk away empty, disillusioned once again.

Always, our greatest, most intrinsic need is to receive what we don't see: the boundless, timeless Shape beyond the shifting-wavering *forms of godliness. The Godness that IS.* Standing watch, hovering, covering, offering the shelter of that Realm where other gods have never dwelt.

A large bird of prey circles above the orchard in great spirals, making concentric loops around the chicken yard. Annie is unconcerned; the chickens are quiet because there is an opaque roof above them. Perhaps the bird is seeking a chink in the defense. But Bea has helpers who monitor the property on essential missions, who help maintain the security and quality of life on Sky Mesa. Cockadoo and girls are safe here.

Annie has her own four-legged, furry predators, and at night she sleeps securely in a smallish mansion with a lock to confound Wile E. Coyote.

Our predators differ; our fears are not all quite the same. Our Father knows each, and he also knows which we fear unnecessarily and which would devour us. I leave my defending to him; it comes, it comes—in time and powerfully.

Our minstrel David said that God *alone* was his rock, his fortress. He would *therefore* not be shaken (Psalms 62, 92). Ah, real security! The Kingdom of God, earth's great sanctuary/fortress, is wherever we invite it, perceive it, and receive it. *We* are privileged to bring it down, within, around us, and by our insistence and persistence and consistent affirmation it remains.

Sky Mesa continues its daily round of life, and one day soon will be a memory. The church will be transformed. The New Jerusalem lies ahead.

The Kingdom will carry on and carry us on forever.

❦ 9 ❦

The designs of humanity

LINDA HAS BEEN CONFINED to her stable and yard today. She reached too far over a fence, and it collapsed. She of course ambled out onto the field and down the road. The fences here are probably forty years old, and many of the patches are patched. A donkey with a yen for green pastures is not much hampered. The fence is, literally, a push-over.

The coyotes know no boundaries here, except the roofed chicken yard, and Annie Goose's apartment. The best of fences cannot forever keep predators out nor inhabitants in. Even Satan's finest, most methodically designed "pens"—Auschwitz, Siberia, all of North Korea, and many others less infamous, have required intensive guarding.

God guards his Temple fiercely from our spiritual pollutions. He guards his borders and borderlands, but lightly, lest our dogmatic souls should pass them by. It is our freedom which draws us over and keeps us—*the fence of our consent*. The Gate is hinged upon this freedom. We may explore to our heart's content his grand domain without fear of dark snatchings. We have, of course, even ventured out—into those bleak byways where adventure beckons and distorts—and returned to lick our wounds and count our blessings.

But the swinging Gate gets heavier the oftener we leave and wander back. We test not so much the largesse of God, the Grace that oils the hinges, as our own disintegrating will. We are bled of strength of character each time we say "Yes!" to darkness, each time we choose the smallness and tightness and meanness that our soul's own sty reveals to us. It is there—it is always there, with its dark shapes rooting around for fodder within us, grunting and shoving and squalling with demand. Their name is Legion, and they come to us as one small, insistent piglet of desire, sire to a host of malignant aberrations.

The Heavenly Host are punctuated around the Kingdom, standing guard at the Gates, waiting to haul us in. But they cannot lift an arm without our *consent*. That is our gift to God, our only Gift, and to withhold it may yet destroy us. *That*, our predator knows full well; he whets his knife upon our suppositions and presumptions and skewers us along these rough scar-lines.

The Kingdom comes; the Kingdom is and ever was and shall be. It is an interval between earth and Heaven, birth and Heaven, *dearth* and Heaven. It is an *inter*vention, an *inter*cession . . . beyond this small *inter*mission. We enter at any point in life where our fences are falling, when the predator is moving upon us.

That is *where* our Gate is. Our escape hatch.

When we are well within the Gate, when we are *well*, within the Gate, we go to Work at mending fences . . . and holding up Light for his Little Ones with their frightened eyes. They will come creeping, as we did, bellies scraped hard from the bark of whatever shaky limb they have crawled out upon.

Linda brays her protest, and pouts against the rusty wire that blocks her. But it will hold. Fences will never stop the predators; their name is Legion.

It is *Light* that will expose them and drive them off.

The road leading up to Sky Mesa is narrow and winding. I can't really search ahead for the ranch to put it into its context with the community.

Now and then I glance up briefly, watching for a bank of tell-tale trees—for it crowns a hilltop. Perhaps it's my flatland eyes, but I see no visible sign of it until, *voila!* —the zig and zag of tracks are there before me. Always it is a sudden bare slash in the ripple of grasses and shrubs. But I know in general where the land is by the birds of prey that circle it, that define a small loop above this shag of hills. The hawks are as visible from beyond as they are when I stand cock-eyed on the premises. Here they hang out; here the pickins are rich, here is wildlife undisturbed and left for the plundering . . . and "take-life" ripe for the tempting. It is an oasis as yet unclaimed by tarmac and cement.

The raptors lead me to the land, and finding access is my part of the hide-and-seek. Perhaps, *aha!,* this is the way it is with God's territory: the "enemy" circling and broaching, swooping in. A veiled entry, an opening that suddenly is there, here, where all was just a sea of weedery before. Of such is the Kingdom of God.

Bea stands leaning on her doorsill and watches, with her own "eagle eye," the swoop and scoop beyond the near perimeter. She has lived for years with this entangled scenario. She is wary as a coyote, despite her equitable ways, and sharp as a chicken hawk. Bea doesn't scurry out with a rifle, albeit she would probably hit her target frequently, acute as she is. Her better answer is protective: *"Know thine enemy."* Know the enemy's motives and moves. Guard the vulnerable, the little ones. Fence them around and above. Feed them safely.

That is essential here, in this small microcosm where daily life is still fundamental—still "real"—a fragile remnant of the ancient balance between mother nature and human nature.

The chickens dart around their enclosure, sharing news and practicing their pecking order. Occasionally a hawk swoops and lands on the wire-fence roof. The squawking is a sudden raucous burst of Knowing our enemy—who it is and why and how and where.

It makes equal sense in the strange new world we dwell in, for we abide uneasily in what has become a great "meat-market," a brazen overlay of scavengers and avengers—ever circling. A mindset of get even or get gotten has morphed us into a state of living that allows, yes, invites mayhem—even though there are rarely causes great enough to kill for. And, conjunctively, this "gotcha" grip raises financial stakes high enough to bring a person, a people, even a nation, to its knees. So often, oh sly as coyotes, the strike is a redressing of injury or the call of "righteousness" . . . the blame or shame game.

The earth today is a roil of cause-conjurers. Strange birds, indeed.

These manipulations range from the clearest and most brutish of motives and practices (tribal enmities and power plays originating from the "bush" or just as likely from an official office). Or . . . the most complex, deceptive, strategically choreographed of take-overs (multi-national corporations, banks, et al). They wing in as "high-minded" deliverers, and there is no imperative for honoring borders, preserving communal well-being, no brokering for a way to live as "neighbors" . . . no cause-and-effect but territorial power and/or aggregation of uninhibited wealth. The Board Room wins because of all the vanities they have pulled from their top hats. Because of the new sterility of life reshaped to nurture our lesser selves.

Always, the lust for power—the endless, timeless greed for *more*. "*. . . War and the rumors of war*" (Matt. 24:6). We live with both incessantly. On small, local (yes, even personal) levels and in an increasingly earth-sweeping upheaval. The toll is incremental and historic. And, of course, the injured must defend themselves! Somehow, any-*how*, at a cost that becomes a choke hold on personal and communal life. *How does a people defend themselves against the driven—with their cloven ways?*

Sometimes, of course, it is not the "driven" who are the perpetrators. Sometimes the chronically injured, who have been chewed upon too long by the hounds of hell, turn upon them. Occasionally intercession comes from beyond. (Without our nation's intervention, the Nazis would have turned their lust into ultimate conquest. A world-altering contingency!)

Whatever the conflict, whomever the victim, retaliating in kind is never the best or only or final answer, of course. The wars of humanity are a great sea of blood, an endless hemorrhage. Our history is a tale of lost causes and unending replications of the "original sin."

No, there is no defense or offense that of itself can resolve such time-less crises. The life of Christ proves out a better alternative:

Don't break the back of the enemy, only his power.

Breaking his power is *crushing the inherent, underlying evil.* Breaking his back is but a temporary "fix" that will not hold. Treaties and covenants lie in shards around our endless broken borders. "Winning" is not merely out-foxing the foxes. It is essentially dependent upon understanding the nature of *our* weaknesses and strengths. The truth of our "ways and means," our brokenness and blindness and fatuities. Knowing our own helps in un-derstanding those of others. It is the primary equipping, the espionage that ranges far beyond the weaponry of man and nation. It is the pivot-point of standing up to evil. This is the first battle.

Fighting our own interior fight and seeing our own corporate dark-ness: This is where the only strength that endures is born. A monumental shedding of all the accumulations of a people's/nation's self-delusions and poverties of living. Jesus calls it "born again." A nation that can change its futile, perhaps deadly course like this is equipped for war. *His kind of war.*

God does not want to break a nation's back. Only its wickedness. First, he has to break our own—bring *us* to surrender before the final war opens.

At that point, we are handed a Sword that is too great to heft in our own small hands until those hands are emptied out. And strengthened to bear a greater load than any enemy can face.

The strength and authority to fight evil as an underlying source is sealed within God's mandate. It is a Given, a discovery, a hidden treasure, a new and rarely coveted understanding. Humanity is not prone to wage war with less than our own best efforts, even if defeat looms like a great, dark raptor. There is no promise of tomorrow hidden in the hollows of victory or defeat.

But there is that Sword of God . . . that mysterious, impossibly absurd injunction that becomes the weapon of choice. *If we know the choice.*

Paul speaks of the "armor of God" (Eph. 6:10-17). The battle gear that protects, and the weapon that defeats: His irrational armor and his preposterous double-edged Sword.

> *"Put on the full armor of God, that you may be able to stand firm against the schemes of the devil."*

Gandhi found it: "*First they ignore you, then they laugh at you, then they fight you, then you win.*"

Martin Luther King followed it. Mother Theresa carried it into the gutters of Calcutta. Many others know this unfathomable power—wherever the mandate of God becomes light, becomes salt. It's a work of moral authority and persuasion of a higher sort.

There is a place for action, a time of unequivocal force, a way of retaliation that has very much to do with Peace-making.

We too seldom find it, this peace-making. All our expediencies, our *piece*-making, dictate other terms to us, as they invariably do. We tend to create wars in the process of resolution. Either instigating physical or material trauma or getting even for what we may well have abetted by our own convoluted actions and reactions is intrinsic to this strange life pattern: All our personal vendettas bundled up and turned into swords of accumulated and tightly focused hatred.

Satan is delighted to step in and point the way. He even tried it on the untried, untested young Man who rose from his baptism in the river Jordan to face the heights and lows on the desert. Jesus showed us something powerful, a frame of reference beyond our hit-or-miss sword-mongering.

After his ordination from John, that amazing baptism, he went directly to the Sinai to dispatch the enemy before the enemy dispatched him (Matt. 4:1-11). Jesus put up a good fight out on the desert without raising a fist. This was a battle of wills, and God won. It was fought on a far different level than Satan was accustomed to, and the cloven one ended up a second-rate strategist. (He always has two left feet in the presence of God.)

When Jesus went into this strange battle (his first of many), he used a weapon we seldom see deployed as weapon: Eternal, bedrock Truth. His Word. The unknown writer of Hebrews also called it a Sword because it severs what is Godly from what isn't.

> "For the word of God is living and active and sharper than any two-edged sword, and piercing as far as the division of soul and spirit, of both joints and marrow, and able to judge the thoughts and intentions of the heart." (Heb. 4:12)

The ultimate weapon, for it emanates only from the thought, the intent, the authority of God. Jesus's mastery of this dynamic was riveting (literally—out there on the forsaken desert where Satan reckoned he would trap this pretender: Stand him high above humanity, invite him to "own" the world he was sent to redeem . . . and watch him reach for it . . . and crash. Pride wins again, even in the very core of God.

Especially, and yes, finally—with God. Eternal retribution for Satan's losing his foothold in Heaven.

Jesus did not turn around and toss the enemy bodily off the pinnacle, despite his power to do so. There were undoubtedly angels hanging around, waiting for an entry point. No, that would have short-circuited God's better plan. *He simply rebuked evil—put it to the test and displayed its poverty . . . and subdued it.* Without flexing a muscle.

Rebuking of this sort isn't your basic finger-shaking, like our parents did. It is a Genesis Work, an elemental act of authority that changes the very course of behavior. That changes the very source of life. That, of course, in some pivotal way, changes the future!

He didn't break the back of the enemy, only his power. He used the evil situation for his good purpose which is far different than our indulging in action for our own advantage.

God's witness demands a response appropriate to his intention here and now. It grabs hold of the spirit of malfeasance and twists it to knots. It is this—not our best-plotted maneuvering, our self-righteous proclamations or fear-driven retaliation—that wins in the end. *Both fluid and fluent, his Truth has an ordination to it that empowers, enacts, enables.* Truth knows the enemy's Achilles' heel. It attacks the very footing of evil. It is engendered by God, within us, to toss the enemy bodily off the pinnacle of their pride.

The secular is always at the mercy of the sacred . . . when you

KNOW it to be so.

When Solomon was confronted by two angry women claiming one indivisible baby, he also spoke such startling Truth. He suggested cutting a child in half. This wasn't "literal truth," which begged murder of an innocent child. But it was an on-site and on-Sight work of God, and the authority and genius of it is still fresh, still with us, exemplary and breathtakingly potent. It was God's witness there and then, and to us even now—his seeing fully and responding singularly—*a startlingly "cruel" directive as the only compassionate answer.* Such power and authority breaks the power of evil without destroying the victim(s). (Too bad Solomon didn't stay with the Source of such amazing discernment!)

God sees as the crow flies. He both sees the crow fly, and sees as the crow sees, flying. Omnivision. He knows every thought of both hawk and dove—he knows who is a danger to whom, and why, and what to do about it. He knew which of Solomon's two frantic women was mother of the child, and set them up for the little drama of disclosure.

There are a lot of things that we know are true—that are right and good, and do not lead us into pits. But there is, above and beyond our varied notions, infinite deception and eternal Truth. This—all of it, evil and Good—is Mystery made manifest. Our Creator, the inscrutable and timeless Truth-Author, portions out whatever wisdom-cum-authority, whatever part of the Whole pertains to whatever situation lies before us. Not situation ethics, but on-site ethicality.

He can shoot predators or build fences, and if he prefers fences while we trust in guns, we'd do well to pause and be sure whose strategy we're following. There is more than one way of destroying evil. God is not inclined to pussy-foot around, mending fences while the enemy is still inside.

He is the author of far more sophisticated "weaponry" than blunt force, however.

The vultures and coyotes of this world are keen and hungry, and they circle our earth-Garden on wing and by foot. We know where the Garden is centered by their presence. And strangely enough, impossibly, to our human reckoning—where the vultures gather we may find our security. It is secured from *within.*

The Kingdom of God is taken by force—by violence—as Jesus told it. Surely and increasingly we know that both the witless and, oh yes, brilliantly contrived violences around and beyond us originate in the fertile mind of the Dark One. They bloom like great fungi across the earth, gnawing down to the core the Fruit of the Garden! This growing plague is greater, more intricate than the designs of humanity! Nothing but the knotted soul of the Prince of Evil could evoke such massive, surreptitious devouring of all that is "normal"—all that has stood the test of the ages, of the better nature of humanity. Without the fierce protection of Holiness, our better nature—our ever-yearning instinct toward goodness, charitableness—is wide open to the wolves of Armageddon. The howl and growl of evil permeates every aspect of life as we have known it.

It comes with a shriek . . . or by a smooth whisper that we strain hard to hear. And so, yes . . . "The Kingdom of God is taken by force." Invisible Force made visible.

Jesus knew what he was saying when he said it. And it is our privilege, as his warriors, to defend it by our knowing *"where"* it exists and *how*—and, by all things timelessly, boldly, powerfully True, good, and just—*why* it exists. It is not *place*, but *placement* that defines this inviolable rest: the internal-unto-external evidence of the mind of God. When we know what that means to us, for us—this great, inclusive certainty—when we "smell" the Kingdom mulch, the composite of his varied and fluid singularities so endlessly-intricately embedded, it is ours to speak for . . . and from. It is ours to defend. Within his sure and secure Perimeter.

We will not break the back of the enemy, only nullify his power.

Bea has gone back inside, back to her routine, knowing that all is well in her surroundings. The crows and hawks have left for now, perhaps replete, and jays wing from sheltering branches of the massive oaks—splattering noisily in the moats beneath the lemon trees. Rejoicing with Annie and the sparrows. And with me.

All is at peace in the Peaceable Kingdom. *Only there,* here.

"In my Father's house there are many mansions."

Sky Mesa has room after room in the L-shaped main building, separated from the house itself by a screened porch at the corner. The rooms are weathered crannies of varied size and purpose—some of which have changed with the years' necessities.

The main house is remarkable and even rather awesome, in a hodge-podge sort of way. It is a large and rambling cavern of dark wood, its massive beams and railroad-tie walls setting a most definitive tone. A south-west *fortress*—bulwark against a hot sun and assorted ravages of time, cool sanctuary from heat and dust and the intensity of these elements and the way they bleach the eyes.

The smaller, peripheral structures are well-made, but their wood has sagged from years of warping. Door and window frames have gone askew. Within the rooms—once bunk-house rooms—everything is slightly off-kilter, a touch decrepit. And wonderful . . . .

Many people have passed through this fortress, this abiding place, through these akiltered doors. Many have stayed a spell, most recently a couple from Liberia who escaped with nothing but their lives. So the fortress is indeed a sanctuary.

We so badly need a safe place in the midst of our turmoil. Seeing these small dramas play out before me is like watching a parable of The Kingdom. Fortress and sanctuary, where defense and rest are equal. He will take us there when we turn to him; when we need defending, he will defend us. We are all so quick to defend ourselves! And so inadequate.

When Jesus spoke of turning the other cheek, I doubt he was advocating debasement. Wimp, hardly! He, and some of his greatest saints, unleashed divine wrath against hypocrisy and greed and pride without unsheathing a sword. He was the *Door*, not a doormat.

Perhaps he turned his cheek to better hear his Father's voice. He said several times, you know, that he could only do what he saw his Father doing.

"Abba, what say You? How do I respond to this bloke?"

Out of this easy acquiescence to a greater Urge than knocking the bloke off his blocks came *power*, authority, *wisdom* that cut like a dagger through pretensions.

That is what I consider *turning the other cheek*. That is what happens when you enter the Fortress for a flicker of Time and come back out to face the blokes and your own block-headedness. God only knows when I *really* need defending, and when I'm simply being defensive. He's quite willing to let *me* know, and to adjust my attitude or to adjudicate—whichever is called for.

This is something I'm learning the long, slow, hard way, of course. I qualify easily as one of the Pharisees, one of the stone-throwers, cloak-holders, the elder brother (sister) . . . and the poorest of the poor, the leper, the widow with her mite, the prodigal with his husky regrets.

Sanctuary is where we come in order to learn which is which—the urge to defend ourselves or the need to be defended. In this great Rest, in the dim, cool cavern of this abiding place, He wipes the blood, sweat, and tears from us, and offers us cleansing and refreshment. Maybe even lemonade . . . .

When I Am Afraid

When I am afraid,
I pull his wings around me—
wrap myself within—
feeling the down of his comfort,
feeling his pinions as a strength
I cannot name. When I am afraid,
the brush of his great Being
washes over me,

and I am small, and still,
and born into a new and clean
conception that is sudden
in its stirring, *here*,
behind my eyes—
before my startled eyes . . .

this tiny embryo of *hope*
that feeds itself so steadily
within the crumbling shell of old despair.

❧ ❧ ❧

The pump-house here was built of rocks of various sizes and shapes and earth-colors.

Another metaphor! I am embarrassed by such a richness, but for reasons I can only guess at, I see them everywhere, and readily give in to them. Life is not in any sense as simplistic as I make it here; but Christ himself soared through parable after parable to explain what we can never fully comprehend, never fully live . . . and what he, whose Mind was fathomless—timeless and infinite—could never fully impart to us muddleheads. And so he drew word-pictures in the air, his voice an opening and a shutting. Like a preschool primer, perhaps. His very life is a metaphor, an unending parable.

Sky Mesa itself is a wealth of parables.

Ergo, the rock pump house. It is a sturdy, unpretentious structure, rocks of every size and shape fitted somehow into a whole—a solid, bumpy-lumpy rectangle that erupts from the rubbled soil as if it heaved up into its own purpose—somehow. Here is my "rock," of course. My own personal metaphor.

When Moses struck the rock for water, he typified a behavior that we humans have indulged in since the Garden. Eve grabbed the fruit; Moses grabbed his trusty rod; both had ignored that still, small Voice and done it their way. Ouch.

God said "*Speak* to the rock."

If Moses thought that he could crack open that hunk of silica like a giant filbert, we'd understand. But he knew God well enough, and God had said *speak* to the rock.

But nooo, Moses was stuck in his old expectations: "*This is the way that God works; it worked this way before. I'll do it right, and to make doubly sure, I'll do it doubly! I'll hit the rock twice, and twice as hard, for twice the water!*"

Moses—who led the Israelites out of bondage and gave them the Testament of YHWH! Moses was locked into his own mindset, finally, just as we all are. We grab a Truth imparted for *his* purpose(s), and slap it on our own circumstance.

We are vigilant in acting. God is vigilant in creating: "*I AM. Ergo, let there be!*" God had shifted gears: Moses hadn't. He ended up with a do-it-himself miracle due to Father's compassion rather than his own righteousness . . . and was blessed that God didn't strike *him* a time of two.

But yes, the rock "complied," and the Israelites stopped crabbing for as long as it took to slake their thirst that day.

Moses . . . ah, Moses, man of great wisdom and vision and faithfulness, paid a heavy price for his one-track miracle. He never made it to the Promised Land.

We are not too keen of ear or understanding or desire either. If God has once said, "*Strike the rock!*" we go on banging at it through the years. We set up the same "relevant" criteria, introduce the most successful formulas (for raising children, tomatoes, or the spiritually dead), prepare the most stimulating packages and proposals, perform the most faithful service.

And that still, small Voice whispers *"No! Speak to the rock!"*

Here, I stand beside the pump-house, running my hands over the jagged, rough-hewn surfaces. I am no Moses. I turn a faucet, and water happens. But I *am* called as a dispenser of Water; we are meant to be something of a pump house, together, I think.

We are called *to* the Water, asked to shelter it, to retain and release it.

We are to stand as a landmark, an invitation, an assurance, letting God gather the water from beneath and above and beyond our knowing and our plotting. If we are open to the Flow, ready to contain it, it comes, it comes—when we speak to the Rock.

The lemon trees are dry again, as brittle as the unfed soul. There is a Fountain that never ceases, meant for such droughts.

Tomorrow I will run hoses and wait beneath the hanging branches for his Water.

⁊ ⁊ ⁊

I found a special rock yesterday. Not that it was ever "lost," or that it had not been seen by other human eyes. But I happened upon it, back behind the house, where it lay in ignobility.

First, it was really a *slab*—a bit of the striation of shale so prevalent here, roughly rectangular, a foot or more each way, several inches thick. I'm no geologist, but it was a fine small slice, nearly smooth on the topside, where it lay snugged in the earth for millennia.

And the face of it was a marvel! A myriad of ancient, tiny squiggles covered it, as if a child had held it clutched, practicing his primal ABC's. Or as if, perhaps, his papa doodled, thinking thoughts too inexpressible to draw coherently.

It was, of course, a bed of wee crustaceans caught upon the floor of some great, shrinking mudhole. They lay under the sun's heated eye, beneath shunting dust and crumbling tumble of rock above. And now they curl here, the brief minutiae of their life etched beneath my hands. The sun's crude Xerox passed its light above them; they are no more than shadow.

And I am tempted to read them, Braille-like, as if that nonexistent child or papa spoke from this small composite. I do not know if fathers and their progeny walked this earth then, trampling on the prehistoric bugs, wading into broad lagoons and squishing living curlicues like these. But this less-than-extraordinary, sun-warmed stone is sacred to me, and I touch its testimony gently. Here lies a fragment of the infant earth, hinting of mortality, proclaiming both our final death and Life. Long, long before we stalked this planet, with our guided spears and nuclear stones, Creation bloomed, the Hand that put this sheaf of stone within my hands was creating dreams of us.

A friend has come to share this day with me. We know this stone is uncovered for us today; it is our treasure. We will love it well, and leave it here, where it belongs. Like small, delighted children, like priests poised trembling at the sill of the Holy of Holies, we build an small altar on the bare earth, placed where the sun will serve to focus its Shekinah. We lay the slab there, faced flat toward the sky, toward the God who carved the instant creatures who have carved their story for us.

And suddenly, simultaneously, we "see" a tablet writ on stone before us—writ cramped from such a large Hand. One great commanding thought passed down from eons long submerged and pressed beneath the shifting earth—repeated endlessly before us and between us and beyond us: *"I AM."*

So there is treasure buried here. Oh, not the kind that you weigh in the assay office, or cut and polish with microscopic precision to its faceting, or melt down for its necessities.

But there is treasure here. Sit with me a moment while the wind rhymes all the varied calls of nature. Here is peace, and continuity, and earth-purpose, and largeness. Here, there is time to explore the hidden regions of the soil and of the soul which we have never found.

୬ ୬ ୬

A spider climbs the post of my rocker. He is so minute as to be invisible beyond a scant twelve inches. What I see of life is much like spider-vision. He measures the arm-width of this chair as I measure the eight-lane freeway beyond my home.

But he is a part of the treasure. His young spider-self is learning to think *web*. When his genes have performed their arachnid calculations well, and his fragile being has come to its full stature, behold—a wispy doily will have linked one small dry stem to another, and it will wait, swaying in the wind's pentameter.

Bees feast on my forearm, betrayed by my scented lotion. I have several small "pin pricks" where they have nibbled (not stung), and it was worth the brief discomfort to watch their busy "hands" and mouths explore me.

They gave up after a few tastes—probably spitting me out in disgust. The bees migrate to my porch from lemon limbs that rumba with the wind. The trees are hung with lemons ripe, lemons hard and tight green, lemons still the promise in a blossom.

Bea comes out to call Annie for dinner, and the magnificent wings spread fully as the goose lifts from her dust bowl. Her voice trumpets hunger and delight, like a ravenous child, and it sounds a martial air above the muted orchard. Twice a day she proclaims the wonder of grain and vegetable scraps; twice a day I am riveted by her raucous exultation.

One of Bea's cats swoops low across the soil, practicing its sleuthing. Its furry underside brushes the prickly weeds, carrying the burrs beyond— an unwitting propagator, thinking *field mouse*.

For some forty-odd years Bea has walked the worn paths from house to barn to shed, while I conducted my wide-eyed explorations of my own small town and moved beyond it. Our worlds come together here, for this brief recognition. We are creatures of a kind, and grant one another some deep legitimacy that each craves and receives lightly. Our intimacy with soil and seasons carves a straight, new path between us, and all this near-half century is one long, variegated season we have known, somehow, together.

It is a *homecoming*, of a sort.

❧ ❧ ❧

The wind blows softly, steadily, from the west, and carries unfounded rumors of rain. Perhaps it comes as promise, perhaps only a mocking reminder of our parched soil and souls. But I welcome it as a Gift, and clumsily invoke it.

This is land that receives rain too seldom—and then in great gulps that it spits back upon itself. The road up here is steep and twisted, and gullied by the wash of rains too sudden and hard to soak to thirsty roots.

Our thirst is like a rasp behind our tongue, a shrinking-up within us where Water wants to be. This great parching is meant to drive us to our knees—dipping into hidden streams, lowering our buckets into secret wells, pleading for rain too long withheld . . . *"like streams of water in the desert and the shadow of a great rock in a thirsty land."*

It "looks like rain" out there. Even the *look* of storm is enough to refresh the smoggy soul a bit. It wings the thought of thunder deliciously near.

Even so, the thought of *Father* brings us freshness. The Kingdom wings across the gulf between earth and Heaven like a drift of rain from clouds passed over. We see them beyond, moving quickly on, but look— some draft of wind, some kindly zephyr has remembered this scarcity of ours, and left us just a promise.

So it is with the Kingdom, which pauses but a Breath-width before us, a Sigh like a sudden shower freshening the sour air.

God has come to us somehow; his stillness moves before we capture it, but there remains a dew.

It is here, in this new clarity, that we *enter in*. His clouds have parted wide enough to draw us forth and on. Here we come to some simplicity, some clean place too foreign to be of our creating; but we are Home again.

From this small and widening Place we see anew. We catch an unspoken Word that drifts over us, that vibrates far beyond our sour hearing. We hear, we see because we have suddenly *become*, somehow.

Now comes a Way to speak, a way to charge, to catapult the frailties that have lamed our spirits. We are on heights now indecipherable. All we know is that we *know* of Grace, and of the homely rod of Justice that he has whittled from his Tree of Life. Our hands are full with new gripping and reaching, with the solid shapes of our mute understanding. From beyond comes thunder and a burst of Light, a promise of deluge and delight.

It suffices.

ॐ ॐ ॐ

The world is speeding up, and I am slowing down. It was inevitable. It's all right, of course . . . mostly. As we grow older, life enhances the quiet ways and shoves away the expediencies that used to shove *at* us. It is good to quiet down, to make pause gladly for the eternal. Now, *here*, I begin to stop and listen to life more often, more carefully, more caringly, and, oh, more freely!

I think we get lost in the great cacophony that pervades on planet earth. Does this sound overblown? Of course, and yet, it happens every day, to all of us.

We vibrate to the whole of life, even in our partial-ness, in our partialities. What is out there pervades. *Invades.* We cannot help it; we are caught up and moved along by the whole—the great, lumbering sum of all the infinitesimal parts. We are one of those small fractions, divided up, broken by the enormities and the sum of all the smallnesses. It is as hard to put words to all this as it is to live with it. *The world*, indeed, *is too much with us*.

And so silence really is golden. We lose our sense of it, of silence as a presence within an absence of external stimuli. It is a near-aberration in an age of "auditory graphics," when all that engulfs the world is poured out upon us by every media, from every angle, for every purpose.

What I am experiencing already in the ragged arms of this small wildness is peace. What is notable is that it is imparted in such a way that it rides with me down the hills toward home. It does not remain behind. This is new, this is *renascence!* Many a sweet retreat of the past has "left me" at the front door, left me bereft of continuity to cling to.

Now I find that joy cannot long hide beneath my hide. It flings itself against the ramparts of my neuroses until they crack. It breaks through every *"Yes, but. . ."* that I have posited. And it squeals with anticipation, cackles with dumb appreciation. The days both here and there and everywhere are full, full, full of slow, sudden, timeless, ephemeral Graces.

The color of a certain cloud passing overhead, the way it makes the sky heave outward by its own nearness. The bray of a lonesome donkey, how she nudges the fence to warm herself at human-side. The sound of a loved voice on the telephone. A peanut butter sandwich, with my back against a rough pepper tree. The way a violin stroked perfectly makes my arms tingle. The warmth of a stranger at the gas pump. A beetle scurrying across my arm, as if I were a shortcut home. The thought of certain friends, and why I love them. So many more. Oh, Graces full, and of an instant! *Kairos!*

> *"Be still and know that I am God! I will be exalted. . . ."*

If his Kingdom is real, it must lie both beyond and within the cacophony. It simply must. And if we are to survive, and to live well within whatever lies before us, we must find it within the silence that lies beneath the noise.

And now I think I need a peanut butter sandwich . . . .

❧ 10 ❧

Like angled stripes

A GRAND OLD PEPPER tree looms before the porch. From its bottom limb hangs an old board swing, its fraying ropes too uncertain to risk the pleasure of testing.

Sometimes I remember how it felt to be young, really young. Actually, I don't have to try very hard; part of me never really grew up. I have climbed a tree or two recently—oh, nothing really high and teetering, no great stretches of hand or foot were required—only a great stretch of imagination.

On my walks here, I have sat in the arms of a giant live oak. Its bottom limb swooped low, barely five feet from the ground. Who could resist its invitation? The second branch was as irresistible, and the next no less so. So I stretched my limbs' credulity, and straddled it, leaning back against the gnarly bark. And I remembered another tree that nurtured me.

I "grew up" in a willow not unlike the pepper trees here. Thus this tree before me is another homecoming. The temptation to try my luck with its heights is often strong, quenched only by the distance to the nearest hospital.

Ah, but I yearn to test that long-neglected swing! I remember what it was like to "pendulum" myself beyond my small stature! My passport to a larger world! The simple up and down, back and forth was every day a new adventure to this small dreamer.

From the mundane wooden board and ropes, hung from the heights of an ancient walnut tree, I catapulted up, up and out—out past known perimeters, out into adventure! I sought every known landmark, measuring the rise in my trajectory by their visibility. From the apex of that ultimate arc came an instant of vision when *then*, and only then, I could see all that there was to see. All the world looked different from that "place." It was mine for a breathless moment.

What was the lure for this small girl-child? Perhaps it was that final great whoosh to the top, where one could never be quite sure if the swing-cum-self would jolt back to possible disaster. Just risk enough . . . .

No, I remember; it was more than that heart-thudding dare. I *wanted* to catapult—to fly over the startled heads of earthbound playmates. Always I longed to see what I could see too poorly from where my feet were planted. Much later I found a word to describe the dilemma:

Epigeal—living on or close to the ground. Yes, I was, we are.

And I guess I know now why I loved to swing. My heart is ever yearning up, up, and out, like a frail pendulum, past my known peripheries, nearly peeking into that great, unknown, unseen Land, that Secret Garden . . . and settling back to where my feet are planted. I can feel the rush of Wind against my flushed cheeks.

I will not fall!

              ॐ ॐ ॐ

When I was a young girl, back in Colorado, our family built a cabin in the high hills, just before the steep jut and jumble of mountains began. We had fifteen acres to roam, up and down, mostly. I was not much impressed by such an acreage; land was "dirt cheap" then.

But it was our family's get-away for about fifteen years. Only a half hour or so from town, it was accessible for an overnight or weekend stay. People didn't venture out on long drives in those days of one-car families and freeway-less travel.

Our cabin was a do-it-ourselves venture, other than the handsome fireplace (which we girls hauled stones to build). We daughters also applied the final touch, linseed oil, on the raw pine half-log siding. It was hard labor, and not exactly a work of architectural art. But it was sturdy and fragrant with new wood and looked out upon glory.

We had two small, spare bedrooms, and a loft where slumber parties begged into noisy being. But the "great room," as it is now being called again (as it was in our great grandparent's day), was where life was lived. It was more family room than living room, and more than that as well. We *encountered* each other, in that expanse, on every level of life. Eating around the old table, piecing puzzles on the floor, sprawling on scarred and faded chairs and sofas—a few or many of us, family and friends.

In God's Kingdom, we encounter each other in intricate ways—in *infinite* ways. We are all of the same family, beyond our disputes, beyond disputing the *yes or no* or *maybe* of it. He calls us into his Great Room, into Blood Relationship that is more binding than any on earth. Nothing— nothing but our act of willfulness can break this brother-covenant.

In his House, we are not all of a kind, only kin. Not of the same mind-set, only the same Mind, which intercedes uninterruptedly between us. This is the great hope upon which the Kingdom is built. Without this Mind of his, we live in a soul-house that is threatened by collapse with every gust, every tap. The proverbial house of cards. His house-upon-the-Rock is our shelter—our invisible sheltering, the center of his Invisible Empire.

It is Here that we think back-and-forth, which is prayer. We curl up on the "window-seat," in the bay window of his Home, with its panorama of Life spread before our inner eye, in that telescopic way of looking which is his. And we lift up to him whatever we see, for his confirming.

Quick images are pressed against our Vision. The sudden shifting of a lens cover, and *click*—there it is, framed for a flick of moment, just long enough, barely clear enough to decipher.

This morning I took a picture of a fence post and ruby geraniums. I got up from my crouch, pleased with the view. When I turned the camera over, I found the lens cover closed. We pray that way often, with closed shutters, not knowing how to pray, what to pray *for*.

From the vantage point of his curvature of window, in my room in this rough temple of his, life looks quite different than from the "darkling plains" beneath. It is all I can count on now in my life—that he has a view-point which I deeply need, and that I must come up to his Place, his holy mountain, to find it.

It is there that we truly meet each other, frame each other with finer focus. It is there that I know you, *really* know you.

I am wealthy beyond words. My Father is a rancher; he owns the cattle on a thousand hills. A most conservative estimate, tossed off just to make a point, of course. He owns the hills and the mountains behind them and the plains and prairies beyond. I have invested heavily in his stock. When

I make requests or state my opinions, I choose to believe I am heard—like the old (and unfounded) E.F. Hutton commercial.

Things are meant to happen when we speak up in his board meetings. They cannot happen without the investment. The old injunction "Put your money where your mouth is!" is well advised. I keep "quiet" a lot more than I used to—or I try to.

When we are deeply enough attached to the ways of our Father, what we say is the Promise, the blueprint of what we get. We create *in kind*. Because my greed has largely been assuaged by his largesse, I am now both concerned with and fired by things pertinent to him. More and more I want what is best for the Kingdom; I am convinced that whatever "it" is, is the best for all parties concerned. A bullish market indeed . . .

I want the Kingdom of God to prosper and grow and pay great dividends and expand into new markets and overpower its competitors, and prove its irresistibility and essentiality and magnanimity and moral strength and *ubiquity*. I want God to corner the market.

SomeDay that will happen. This I know.

This is all I know: It is not an event to fear, but to desire with long and secret and steady fervor. Not to manipulate, to massage, to devise/revise and spin and cook books and "rob Peter to pay Paul," if both Paul and Peter bet their livelihoods on a flawed premise . . . built their lives on false premises.

The incredible elasticity of God's substance is unimaginable here, where and Power and Money rule. We have all the power of the universe, all the coin of the Spirit, amassing before us infinitely. In The Kingdom, *only* in The Kingdom, there are no golden calves.

I have found my birthright. I am part of the Greatest Enterprise this side of Eternity—*Corpus Christi*. It offered stock when it went public 2000 years ago.

The Lord God fed the Israelites on the desert. He is still feeding, selling off a herd or two from his undiminished stock. He is still enlarging his holdings, outwitting his competition, buying up rights to our shoddy souls, paying off old debts incurred by his new depositors.

It works. Somehow, line upon line, precept upon precept, we find out that this Kingdom is everything . . . everything.

Jesus said, "I have food and drink that ye know not of."

I know where he got it.

꙳ ꙳ ꙳

Time is compressed here, or so it seems. The three days I spend at Sky Mesa are not so long a time (from Monday morning until Wednesday evening), but there is a Timelessness here. Call it TimeFullness.

Every week I have a break, a "company" break—a neighbor, or a friend from the city who needs a get-away. We break the bread of Rest together.

Things tend to look different from this front porch. This run-down little acreage gets under my heart and starts nudging, expanding exponentially. The things I left behind do not shrink—oh, no! They simply measure differently, as if laid against some new breadth, and take on new dimension.

Time itself covers everything differently for me now. *Covers*, I say emphatically. I've long known that *"a day is as a thousand years"* and vice versa. But the evidence has mounted on this long porch. There is time, in the Kingdom, for things to gestate, to root and sprout and bloom . . . between now and the next phone call. There is also time for things to, perhaps, die a quiet death—dreams too faded, too long held in darkness; hurts and hates and other ancient hauntings.

That's the way it is in *Kairos*, God's appointed time. It is, really, Time Anointed—by the God who could send out a universe on a flicker of thought. A long, long instant! Why should I be surprised at the way Time lingers here as Cover? Or that a day is as a fortnight?

Things don't collapse in the Kingdom. What does that mean? I'm not sure, except expansions generally do, at last . . . collapse. But the Kingdom of Heaven is not froth; its reality is undiminished by our tangled "truths." *"The substance of things hoped for."* Substance invisible, evidence of those tangibles just beyond our comprehension. We do not have to pretend, or portend. It comes, whatever Bread he breaks before us in this long flicker of TimelessFullness.

If it is ours, it is worth waiting for, worth working for. The work goes on within, a silent listen/respond that hovers like a Benediction over our small pastures.

The Kingdom is that Tree full of fruit both green and gold, and blossoms both full and tight, of dark, dusty leaves and new pale-green leaves beginning. All are right on time, as I am.

Under the Tree of Life is a moat filled with Water—and, I hope, a big gray goose splashing.

❧ ❧ ❧

Tonight I am propped up in the big oak rocker, which I drag out to the porch every morning, back in at sunset. It has a touch of arthritis, like me.

This was a different day. Once again a friend came to spend it with me. I parcel out my time here with great care—it has taken me a life time to arrive, and the near-solitude is a solstice of sorts. A time of passage from life to Life, light to Light. I am being changed from day to Day.

Years ago, as a mother of young children, I would have "died" for this time, this experience. It would have meant something much different then. Rest, yes, but not of the sort I have sought this year. My on-hands mothering days are over; my Sabbath is a deeper well to draw from now, lined with a crush of rock and years of sediment.

Vesla sprawls across the coffee table next to me, across my papers, around my books, knowing they are important enough to nap upon. Cats bestow themselves so—favoring us and our personal effects with their being. There is a touch of noblesse oblige to it.

I hunted down the hurricane lamps and made plans to light them. It seemed like a proper atmosphere for night-writing. But it is contrived, I realize, simply to add an atmosphere. It would also add pollution, and with my degree of "eptitude," the fire department would probably end up here to save the remains.

No, Vesla and I are happy with the evening and its cricket calls and Mozart on tape. This small corner of creation lies blanketed in rich, country smells and sounds, and it wraps around me like benediction.

I wish I could give this time apart as gift to whomever needs it. Nearly all of us do, for many reasons. Tonight the sense of lovely isolation, a strange semi-loneliness that I would not break, surrounds me.

The world grows more frantic in its search for space and place. We buy ourselves off with lesser satisfactions; we do the best we know to do to meet that need. But there are no substitutes for the simplicities that heal us.

Vesla washes, stretches, jumps down to her kibble bowl, comes back to groom again. My papers grow more rumpled, and some day, when she is only a half-remembered image, *cat*, my rumpled papers will bring her back to me—Vesla and this room and its lights and shadows and Amadeus and his cricket chorus beyond.

A great simplicity . . . .

❧ ❧ ❧

There is one barren mountain in the near distance, beyond my perch on the porch. A landmark in this east county, it's hulk is visible in snatches through the orchard, its crown caps the trees like a carapace. Varied strata lie like angled stripes across its surface, describing its "journey" to those who can read such "maps." Hunched around its base, lesser hills wait with it in this motionless voyage through time.

These hills are not all that old. But they are full of history; humankind has left early marks upon this dusty, dusky land.

This morning, a bevy of hawks circles above, rowing the currents, eyeing the ground for small signs of life. They play on the wind, as they ever did, before our kind was here to watch.

This land has not always existed; I need to remind myself of that. There were no coyotes, no mountain cats, no bronzed men striking flint from the granite cliffs beyond me. There were no lemon trees, no hawks floating, no gray geese, no Sky Mesa, no me.

Were I an atom in God's archive, or a thought in his great heart, I was never the *me* of this earth. But I am here, in this twilight time of life as we have known it. I am called, was called forth, across the span of Infinity, and Fathered by an impulse far greater and more loving than my own father's act of love. I *believe* this now, irrevocably—for me, for each of us.

When I met my Father, I knew it.

A memory from the past, words that I've never forgotten: When Bobby Kennedy was murdered, the electronic billboard of a local shopping center held a brief, startling message: *"There are not, nor ever can be, any accidents with God."* Does this sound harsh? It might if we don't embrace the nature of God as Father and our *being* here as a gift carefully held.

The message-maker (the development owner) was not blaming God for Kennedy's death—divine retribution for some secret sin(s). No, he was stating the obvious: God knows *all*.

From the moment of our conception he tracks us with a yearning eye, watching our life fork off, converge with this and that, this one and that one (whom he also tracks, with the same great grip of yearning). He waits before us at each blind corner, pointing out quietly his bright alternatives to our dark or bleak wanderings and wonderings. Some of our "convergences" are blessed, some a brush with evil.

Our departure is writ upon his slate.

Bobby passed beyond us harshly, as did his brother, and Martin Luther King, and too many others through the years. We can ill accept such mean departures. The world goes on beyond them, without them—but not unchanged, oh no!

There are no accidents of birth or death in his Kingdom. God is "born" with us each, and "dies" with us when we die, whether it is too soon or a timely passing, or we are drawn too thin by the length of hard years. His *idea*, which we are, and were to become—the expression of Life which is us—is too dear to call back lightly. Love does not forfeit, nor forget. Even the "least" of us! Perhaps especially the least among us, the constant tear in his eye.

YHWH: I AM THAT I AM. The mystery whose Name the sages of Jerusalem dared not speak aloud. Love beyond love, extravagance which can never be ciphered or deciphered! But *YHWH* is also a God of sacrifice. His Son did not linger long among us.

Our history, our histories, are not random, not at the mercy of a hair-trigger. Perhaps these two notable brothers gave up this brief domain to alter history in some way unimaginable. Perhaps the dark convergences that robbed them of their right to live out their heritage was something Known and slipped into history beyond our puny comprehension. I choose to believe this.

No, there *are* no accidents with God. In his Kingdom, we are not expendable—none of us. Each cell in our bodies, each hair on our head has been plotted, coded with our DNA. (Some of us would like to talk to him about quantity over quality!) We are focused, each, in the center of his Seeing Eye, carried in his great knowing, his recognition. When we fall, it is not to dust, but into trust, where nothing accidental can betray our life.

We are his sparrows. An unimaginable Truth that we cleave to because we have been *told* by that still, small Voice which was once unimaginable also—the Voice that launched a universe and bespoke Life.

Cockadoo has become a father! Probably a week ago, all unbeknownst to me, in a box of straw in this humble hen-house, one more chick-let came into the world. I wasn't here for any proclamation.

The baby follows its mother like a tiny shadow, scooting after her on its tiny fidget legs, like a little wind-up toy of itself. It is *imprinted* on her—bonded, received of and receiving her—role model as she is to this bit of fluff and sprouting feathers. She is teaching it how to live, to adapt to life in this small arena.

Chickadoo has its father's wings already. Whatever its sex and coloration, its other markings—for mama and dad are certainly dissimilar—it *does* have its father's wings. Cockadoo has left his mark upon the child, and one cannot deny its parentage.

I wonder if my Wings show yet? I wonder if my Father crows with pride and joy over me? This question gives me a moment's pause, as it should. Bernard de Clairvaux said, *"What we love we shall grow to resemble."*

Whatever my own self-assessment, I suspect that the nearer and dearer Truth is that Father does indeed proclaim the wonder of me—simply because he has Fathered me, sired me, birthed me, not once, but twice! Chickadoo did not ask to be born. He/she was an unwitting expulsion on an unremarkable morning by a rather nincompoop hen.

Unlike God's very Son, we did not ask to be expulsed into this world of grief and glory. But I—I chose to be re*Born*! I asked for asylum, for a Truce between Heaven and my ruined earth. I climbed into the yolk of his mind, curled to an embryo and lay within him. I am perhaps a small bit of fluff, but I was Born with no other imprint than his great marking upon my soul. I have his Wings! I think he knew how many times the cock would crow for me, as for Peter. Perhaps it could happen no other way—without my fidgeting legs and peeps of fear and protest, my running feet and my denials.

The thing is, he counts it all joy that we say *"yes!"* to entering the Womb on this, our seventh day. We are laid down to rest in darkness and hatched into a Light we never knew was there, a nestling-place we never found in all our searching.

Someday, maybe not too far removed, perhaps the sky will split with a mighty crow of Thunder, and we shall lift our chicken-little heads and raise our startled wings, and the Wind shall catch us up.

For we have our Father's strong and lovely wings.

The earth is altered, stone upon stone, by forces within its rocky ribs. Our world is altered, moment by moment, life upon life, by each thought, gesture, act of kindness or rage of each of us. The silent hills have stood, striped with their ancient history, while we humans have come and gone beneath their shadows. The strata of our life here endures as well, etched across earth's history.

Once more I trace the lines across the rugged face of this middling mountain. It reminds me of an old chief, locked in reveries and histories we will never know. Like the first people who dwelt beneath it and scaled its heights to search the far horizon and to speak to the Great Spirit, I too search beyond it for a wider vision. The mountain does not stand isolated. It is defined not only by what it is, but by everything around it. In the center of lesser mounds, it rears its strangely vulnerable head. Among the Rockies of my heart-land, it would be lost, but here it is a landmark.

And you and I, small sparrows on a phone line perched—we are here today, gone forever. Eagles and sparrows, mountains and the cycling fruit trees now spread before me; all have their short or lengthy moment in this parenthesis we dwell in. Next, we climb a higher hill to view what lay behind us and face beyond.

Hawks circle the hills and the sparrows dart among the cycled fruit trees. Spread out before me, God's own sacred landscape, which I have always dreamed was waiting.

It is no accident which brings me here.

இ இ இ

Who said *"God must love sparrows; he made so many of them"*? Quite a few of these cheery gray busybodies inhabit this domain, despite a half-dozen resident cats and other prowlers. The birds flit beneath the soaring hawks and flapping crows, bounce upon small branches and phone wires, spreading their common chatter with crisp staccato from perch to perch. I like to watch them. I think God does have a special penchant for sparrows.

Perhaps late on the fifth day, his paint pots all but empty, daylight fading, he simply spattered earth colors over two small clumps of clay, and released sparrows into the sunset. A constant backdrop to the vibrant wings and beaks of his exotic species. They are a good foil for sunsets and macaws and peacocks.

Whatever fancy says, I see the sparrow as our scriptural brother-in-feathers. I think God sees our flitting around, in and out of range of his voice, in and out of range of predators, as quite sparrow-like.

I hop from wire to twig to fence post with both a whim and a will. We *are* restless creatures, aren't we? I watch the doves and pigeons poise in near *in*animation, like decoys fixed upon a high point, a lure and a warning. Crows preen and glean with some innate precision, a fixation, as if they were key-wound and released. But sparrows are *my* equivalent.

They are not stupid birds, simply unadorned. Their beauty is of the "plain people," the Shakers and Amish, the Quakers of old, who are lovely in their stark outer simplicity, their dress and demeanor and life style.

Sparrows are such. Beneath the plainness, perhaps their hearts are aburst with *joie d'vivre*. I think sparrows have more fun, more simple pleasure in being, than we can know . . . just like their human counterparts.

Sparrows are meant to proliferate, to keep the wild beauty of nature in balance, to even out the raptors' grip upon life. So it is with us; those of splendid color and shape dominate; sparrows *pre*dominate. Their feathers are muted, but not their voices! They reign by their charm, their song, their sheer ubiquity.

His Eye is upon us. If we have the wings of eagles, the view is great from the heights. But sparrows see much more of life in its intimate detail; they are more nearly "down to his earth." They describe us well.

> Jesus *"had no stately form or majesty that we should look upon him.*
> *nor appearance that we should be attracted to him."* (Isa. 53:2)

Our Father sent us his own from among such a flock.

ೂ ೂ ೂ

I made a loop around the ranch early this evening, when the sun began to slip into its envelope. Nature is rich and pungent at this time of day. A neighbor's dog joined me and we sniffed out the territory together. I have done this many times, in these more than eighty days.

"Around the world in eighty days."

I have been nowhere, here—tucked away on this small shelf of earth. Why do I feel so *traveled* now? It seems as though, it feels as if I have traveled further here than life has ever taken me. I am almost embarrassed to admit it—that I am so, ummm, readily satisfied.

Around the world . . . I remember, early in this journal, expressing my yearning for adventure. What of the Jungfrau and the craggy heights of New Zealand and the depths of the catacombs and the breadths of the moors and savannahs? What of them indeed! Ah, someday, perhaps. Probably not. But it's all right. Maybe it's as much a matter of attitude as latitude.

Living . . . I suspect it's where we go and what we do within us, far more than the space we occupy. But of course! That's really what life is, oh foolish woman. I've always "known" that. We all "know" that! We just don't "do" it.

Running away . . . we are forever running away. Which is different than exploring.

Perhaps we don't discern the difference between *running* away and *getting* away. Maybe that's one reason we are such a problem to each other. I can admit now (ah, hindsight!) that I could have "gotten away" long before I came up here.

Some years back, my publisher's wife invited me to spend nearly a week in Vail, Colorado—in a beautiful four-story home in a very exclusive area. It was a dream vacation. It was a lovely gift. And I came home still dragging *me* behind me.

I guess I have learned something about all my/our comings and goings. Aside from the natural desire to see the world we inhabit, to somehow make it more ours, and ourself more *its*, there is that strong urge to *get away from it all*. I think I was right about my *wanderlust*. A better word for this need is probably *Lebensraum*. Space to live. *"Gimme some space, man!"* It became a cliché long before today.

We need *living* space desperately. Oh, not just those among us who endure life in squalor or are rubbed raw in elbow-to-elbow proximity. It is, of course, not a matter of square feet or even, primarily, of privacy. Mansions are no better, not for *living* room, not for the kind of space that is like air in our lungs. Certainly it is not a matter of luxury.

We know this! It is more a matter of faith. Gut faith.

> *"Let us all come forward and draw near with true (honest and sincere) hearts in unqualified assurance and absolute conviction engendered by faith, (that is, by that leaning of the entire human personality on God in absolute trust and confidence in His power, wisdom and goodness). . ."* (Heb.10:22, Amplified Bible).

Jesus was crowded in by a world that pushed and pulled at him incessantly. He had "no place to lay his head." Direct quote! What he did have was an interior landscape that was his own wide space to dwell in. His own. No one could disturb or distract him there; nothing could persuade him to leave it, because there dwelt the ONE he lived for/with.

"He shrank from the horrors of separation from the bright presence of the Father." (Heb.5:7b)

Toward this Presence we travel, or from him we run. Away from The Hound of Heaven* who pursues us in all our escapism.

We are looking for a place to rest; he offers us simply a way of rest. A get-away in the midst of it all. When we stand still, within, we catch up somehow; we give some things and people, and God, time to catch up with us.

Sky Mesa Ranch . . . this is probably no one's dream location. For some, it would be a place to avoid. But, oh Father, it has become for me a place to dream!

Now, I guess I can *walk toward*. To what? To whatever's out there.

I've been around the world and back. I'm ready.

⁂ 11 ⁂

Illuminating the cutting edges

A SCATTERING OF LEAVES from the overhanging pepper tree drifts across the porch; a cluster of its dried berries crunches beneath my bare feet. They release their pungency, a sharp smell that I associate with Southern California.

Peppers are nearly ubiquitous in this neck-of-the-woods. I love them for their durability, their awkward beauty, the evocation of plenty in the midst of want.

The mornings are slower now. I spend most of my time looking around, touching things, picking and pressing leaves—the tangibles, memorizing what intangibles I must take with me, filtering through the weeks past for images that must not be left in the clutter that pervades here.

When I look back, weighing the *sum* of these three and a half months, I see how heavy it is with significance, and how aLight it is. I suppose most of our comprehensions are back-lit. (Lit *in relief* and *with relief*, a bad word-play, comes to mind. I am guilty of many such. . .)

Isn't it true? When back-lighting reveals the hidden dimensions of our pain, illuminating the cutting edges, the flaws, the depth-*mis*perceptions, the shallows . . . ah, new perspective! It is not, maybe, such a dragon after all—or perhaps more a paper dragon? An inflated one, blown out of proportion?

But maybe behind that great inner distortion lurked a real beast, in hiding.

And if the beast *was* real, was heavy, was scaly with the hellish hide we fear so, then it is good that we see it now for what it was and is. The weapons are now, somehow, commensurate— both lighter and weightier. And oh, far more real!

Here, on this rough tableland, Time has ceased to be my enemy, a dragon that devours, a beast that breathes a smoke screen over past and future.

In the Kingdom, the dragon is a chameleon after all.

వ్ వ్ వ్

It has been uncomfortably hot and humid the past two days. Throwing open doors and windows (screens are less than whole here) has invited in all sorts of wee, flying entities. A few of them made their familiar whine around my prostrate body all night long. They seemed to prefer my O+ blood over whatever type keeps my guest-friend alive and perking. I didn't perk until after the coffee did this morning.

What keeps me chugging along, mostly, despite the whine of small distractions and the itches of uncertainty and certain nibbling doubts, is relationships that are like mine with my Father—familiar and forever new. The *thrust* and the *trust* of them.

I was watering and grooming the geraniums when my friend's car pulled up out back. Today's visitor and I go back "a ways" for Californios. We've been writing for over twelve years, solo and together, in the same guild. We often pick up on our themes and dreams at about the same time. It feels good to bounce things back and forth and know that there is enough communion between us that we can slice through all the peripherals and get to the core.

We challenge each other. We can do it without concern for scraping off veneers, for we know where the core is, what it is, and how deep a deepness we have to work with. We know about Water, where the other is concerned. If we don't, we can ask. We know when there is something rotting at the core; we can tell that, too. The trust is there.

Most of us, not knowing each other, circle around warily, afraid to take the plunge. It's a hard thing, really, and sometimes we end up jumping in where angels fear to tread. But that's a small price, really, for seeing God at hand, at work.

My friend and I learned it, over the years. We found our landing spots, as I did with others. You could say our small acres "adjoin." Enough of the same things grow there that we can identify them, name them, bless them.

But it is the variations that make it work.

My garden could never be mistaken for that of my friend. I bloom with wild and tangled images. Her fruit grows from different soil, from a different mulch. It has her "character." This dear one sprouts a heady mix of short, vibrant truths that make a pungent potpourri.

Another beloved one is an early garden; I coax roots up through the barren soil of her background, and even now I see buds she only dreamt were there. Cup by small cup, she waters what is hers today.

Another friend is the tangy, sun-warmed smell of the desert in spring. All are the good earth to me. One of my dearest has left for our Promised Land. Surely she is the rich scent of autumn on the wind—burnished with the red and gold of all our yesterdays and tomorrows.

And how could I have survived these past lean years without my several brothers-Given? They have loved me with a seeing Eye and discerning heart. Surely God will reward them for their patience, their insistence upon God's best for me. May they reap a thousand blessings!

What we are to each other as friends becomes our pruning and our blooming. If we dare to garden seriously in our prized relationships, we will take risks. The sudden winter chill, the devastating heat, too little or too much rain, a pulling back unwarranted or unexplained, a riot of conflicting emotions that are a haunting between us. And, yes, many little foxes lurk! But oh, the Gardens we may tend between us! We know only what is given us to know of our own soul-soil, and cannot know each other well enough to measure roots and fruit—not until the ripening, ours and theirs. Gardens are for pleasure and profit. The profit is in the pleasure; the pleasure becomes the often inexpressible profit.

The world needs befriending, one upon one, for we cannot love greatly until we learn to love small-ly those whom we know and must or choose to live with, right now.

For richer or poorer, or both, in ways we all are.

❧ ❧ ❧

It is September. Summer is all but gone, but the Southern California skies are bright and hot. Only the leaves know the season of the sun's slant upon them; they fade to gold and brown, faking autumn beneath our tropical skies. And we beneath the skies—we fade to a dun-colored sameness, yearning for the crisp glow of Fall.

I am watering the orchard again, probably for the last time. My tenant-friend returns home next week, and I prepare for an unexpected joy—a gift undreamt of a few short weeks ago: My husband and I are moving to a new home in a mountain village even further from the city than this rustic spot! And, stunning in this debt-ridden age: *we are trading houses!*

I am amazed at the miracle of this sudden coming-together between two "unsuspecting" couples, the instant knowing of what was to be.

I don't know what it all means yet; it is too soon to weigh it. I can only accept it with a deep sense of wonder. What I do know now is that the city is no longer mine; I am no longer "its." I have spent a quarter century caged, not unhappily, within its growing perimeters. (Oh, Goosie—I am out with you now!) And this time of retreat has been a weaning away from a quarter century of urbanity, of "civilized" pleasures and frustrations and attitudes. I had to see myself, my life, differently before I could live it differently.

It is hard to uproot, even when one's heart is all full of other dreams and needs. There is a grieving, a true loss in every step ahead. The shedding and shredding within sometimes seems too great to risk.

I am called back constantly by loves and lures that speak more loudly than that still, small Whisper. But he *has* spoken, and we both know it. That is enough to mend the seams of faith.

Our ties to the city are not to be broken. They will stretch. But our lives, in a sense, are to be broken—severed off like a twig, perhaps, and grafted, rooted, in this hilly soil.

The Kingdom of God has opened before us . . . .

ช ช ช

Vesla sits beside me here, purrfectly content. I come and go in her life, and she accepts me with equanimity and affection now. She will undoubtedly do as much and more for her "mother" next week.

And soon I shall sit, a bit *im*perfectly content, I suspect, in new surroundings. I have come to a final understanding in my final week here, at this "broken-down" ranch: It is my own brokenness which was the greatest gift. It brought me here, where I have belonged for this small paraphrase of Time.

We belong nowhere and in all places; we are forever strangers and forever at home in this unruly, lovely world. We belong to God, and to ourselves, ultimately, and we serve each other, need each other, bless each other as best we know how. God is in the middle, in the center between it all, holding it all together, sanctifying and satisfying it.

He, not place, is the Centeredness of life. He chooses; I follow. A bumpy road, at times. *Not a level path . . .*

My knees and soul are scarred from falling, but I hope I bend more readily now. This is to be my new "lot" in his Kingdom. And so I yield to this new, small and unforeseen oasis beyond me, which is a dear, but paler micro-setting of my treasured Rockies—that dear, pale counterpart of his glorious Heights.

This is my new lot in the Kingdom of God, in each sense of the word. I could not have come to it without coming *here.*

It is a present joy to contemplate contemplating the night sky and that huge splatter of stars that are veiled beyond the city lights and smog. It is a gift too dear to describe. The wounded howl of coyotes, the hawks circling, jays thrashing the air, a wind full of scents I had almost, but never fully, forgotten—oh, no, never *really* forgotten . . .

Perhaps I have paid a price for this new treasure, in some ways, but it will be a gift nonetheless, and I can only accept it with awe and unshakable gratitude.

❧ ❧ ❧

Hello, world! I greet you from atop this smallish hill on a mesa in the great Southwest. I am coming back to you, coming back yet moving on.

And his last Gift to me here: This sudden memory.

All too many years ago, upon a larger hilltop in the Rockies, I stood like this. I was twelve years old, and I was looking out at the seemingly endless ranges beyond me. Looking out at life. As I have been here . . . .

I felt a "tug" at that moment that defied my comprehension. It left me weak-kneed and giddy. I didn't know what to make of it, that great burst of yearning, that sense of foundness and identity that had no real focus. I was shallow, I was petulant; I was ignorant—especially of the ways of God. The Holy Spirit, to me, was a perhaps-fictional gray "something" that dwelt in the tents of the Israelites and smote them now and then.

All I knew in that moment of utter clarity was that *I would write—that I must write and write . . .* and that I would never live out the small drama of my life to its meant conclusion unless I confessed it *now* (then, that moment) from that mountain top. *It must be pronounced before it escaped me!*

Why? I couldn't have told you then; perhaps I know better now, after all my flailing away at life.

Doña Quixote . . . But I knew this much—that it was an annunciation that I must seal while it was upon me.

And so I hollered it out, this "'mandate"—with all my childish hyperbole, of course—feeling quite foolish, wondering if some puzzled resident might pause in astonishment beneath a tree on a nearby acreage. But it felt like *power*, and something like the wonderment that comes on Christmas Eve when one is small and still convinced of elves and prancing reindeer.

I yelled it out to the forest, and to the mountains beyond the mountains, and to the years beyond my few years. I knew by my body's sudden heat and the coolness in my soul that something wonderful had happened and that I would always, *always* remember this day.

And then I went back down to life as it was, and quite soon, I admit—if not immediately—I forgot that mountaintop moment. Probably it was not to *be* remembered. For all this life-time, that Moment has been buried beneath the tumble and jumble of living.

Until now. In a sudden cataclysm, in an earthquake of sorts within, it has been given back to me whole. Whole and completed . . . the smell and sights and sounds and colors of that experience are as real to me as if I were young and there once more. The scuff of my tennies, the feel of a pebble in one shoe, the stripe of the long-forgotten shirt, the dried moss on the tree next to me, the warming air, the cloud of gnats that spritzed around me. My noisy breath, and the way my broken voice broke the calm . . . and unknown to me, oh yes, broke my childhood.

> Charles Swindoll said, *"Your brain contains a permanent record of your past that is like a single continuous strip of moving film, complete with a soundtrack from your childhood on. You live these scenes from the past, one at a time, when a surgeon places a gentle electrical current and applies it to a certain point on the temporal cortex of your brain. You also feel exactly the same emotions as during the original experiences."*

Think of that. The Great Physician touching my temporal cortex.

Could it be that the human race will be confronted with this irrefutable record at the Judgment of God? Judgment of God-in-the-making? Rather a beginning; I was going on thirteen. Perhaps it was *bat mitzvah* up there, mountain-high, for this small, a bit pudgy, more than unspiritual Anglo Saxon *goy.*

But something changed in me after that summer afternoon—something that I never really understood until *this* summer afternoon. A restlessness that nothing ever stilled. *Until this very day.* Now I have come home in a way that has nothing to do with location.

This is where the *Kingdom* is for me now. This is *what* it is for me. It is finally *my* place. The words I called out then echo now like a fresh wind. They are writ large upon the walls that have constrained me. It is enough to know that the moment upon that hilltop so many years ago was never lost to me and was for his season waiting.

I am satisfied. It is well with my soul . . .

Like the barren mountain in the view before me today with its crags and rubble and the strata of its ancient thrust revealed, I see my life revealed before me. Not just the rubble, but the solid shape of it.

I stand here, looking out, as I did so many years ago, feeling that same old/new trembling within, that sudden weakness in my legs that tells me I am on holy ground.

I can only wonder . . . .

❦ 12 ❦

Vast and simple and homely

THESE WISTFUL, REST-FULL DAYS are behind me now. My retreat into a world not my own is all but over. And yet it is neither over, nor not my own. I have staked out a claim that will forever be mine. What I take with me is more than soil and sun and beasts of earth and sky.

I have gone on a long journey here (fifteen short miles from town), and come Home in the midst of it—have found the way *into* and *out of*, and it is all the same. Oblique? I suppose so, but it is something that only such journeys beyond Time clarify.

Life goes on, and we go on, or not. Maybe that's the wisdom I have lost, or never truly found—to see that continuity is more a gift than a deduction. I am not lost. The years ahead, or days, perhaps, are a discovery. What is lost is picked up down the road in other dimension, in other connotations.

It will all come back, all that is mine, to greet me, not to haunt me. *Kairos*, he calls it.

In a sense, I know no more now than those few months ago. Nothing has changed . . . and everything has changed. I am changed. I have been knocked off my premises. It is humbling to face the universe, the universal, straight on. I have found that the earth stays on its course despite my flagellations—despite my lashing out and lashing down.

We do that. We so intensely equate all life with the struggling and the groping, the whittling and paring and padding of our own souls. The equation doesn't work; we are too fractioned by our partialities to discern the whole of *who we are*, in the midst of the great sum of living. Our divisions and additions inevitably betray us.

We live in a smallness, in a lie.

Comes the Kingdom . . . and suddenly our divisive ways and the old restated, reshuffled formulas we have taught ourselves are insufficient. It's all so much greater, and simpler, than our small profundities.

Life is meant to be a multiple—a multiplicity of new perceptions. This is the simple complexity of the Christ breaking bread and fish, offering the loaf and wine . . . breaking down his seeing and his blood and his cells to new Creation. Multiplying all out of proportion.

"I am the Bread of Life," he said.

There is new purpose sprouting now in everything I do—more so in some ways than others, but I purpose to play also, as I do life's work. I have learned to play as well as, as heartily as I labor. I have been, here, as a child in his meadows and courtyards. Living in Truth.

The Kingdom has come for me in the midst of the turmoil I have dwelt in. God has broken off a bit of his landscape and planted me here/There, laid it over the dry and somewhat ugly and wondrous nooks and crannies of these scarred hills.

I have shared space with a wise woman and a sway-backed donkey and aged goose and a scattering of chickens, and all their peripheral landscape. I have dwelt with spiders and bees and fed with them upon his resources. His Truth has come forth like water from the old pumphouse, gushed into sudden ponds beneath the knotted trees. It has been messy, and neat as Truth is neat—in those vast and simple and homely ways that our heart always knows.

I will never return to quite the same spot; certainly Sky Mesa Ranch as I have known it will soon be changed. But it is forever there, unlike that fabled Brigadoon . . . as his Garden, great Truth beyond its uncertain borders, is forever there.

Only when we find our Home, the Kingdom of God, in this crowded, lonely earthGarden, will we fully be "found," and fully find each other, and begin—perhaps, at last—to live well here in this fragile Ark.

I would, indeed, wish this time and place to everyone.

Linda, Annie Goose and Cockadoo, and all the feathered denizens here are yours.

You need to know a Bea and her history, the enduring mystery of her being here—and cherish her fine stubbornness and frailty. You need a Kingdom where a unique young person shares this rugged space in it in order to save, in some way, spaces far beyond it. Awkward? Life is as awkward as that thought, as entangled as my syntax. Sometimes it comes out that way. But it all makes sense, somehow, within his Borders.

You, each of you, need a Kingdom-of-God-place—a Sky Mesa—*some-Place* to go to within when your soil is baked and cracked with drought and there is no water, no cloven clouds on your horizon. May you find your way to it. May he lead you there! For you it will be smaller or larger, greener or hillier or flatter, a back lot or back country or back bedroom, alone or not. But within its fluid borders lies your Promised Land. It's all there inside you, waiting.

If I could gather you here, one by one, for one long flicker of God's time, and settle you upon the porch rocker with a mug of tea or fresh-ground coffee, I would point out, ahead of you, all the strange-familiar beauty of this Landscape that I see.

And you, as I, would breathe a vast, long sigh, and *know*—for always and ever—that this is what we are seeking, always and ever seeking, and that now we have found it. Now we are found. Now we are Home.

Sky Mesa Ranch is ours, forever ours.

Postlude

THE KINGDOM COMES. IT comes to us when we are laden down with insecurities and dissatisfactions, when we are fractured at our strongest places, all weak-kneed and strong-opinioned. It comes when we are doubled up with grief, double-minded from our doubts and desires. The Kingdom comes like a tickling thought, or a trickling Word that makes its small erosion over and over until the bank of earth we cling to is washed away.

Oh, the Kingdom comes; it must! We have held it back, dammed and damned it with hesitations and our heresies, blasphemed it with our vast pretensions and pettinesses, coveted it without the Grace of yearning, without the simple *Ahhh!* that carries us across its ramparts.

The Kingdom comes. The proclamation thunders boldly against a sullen sky; there is no denying it! We can only watch and wait and open up our rankling souls, dry buckets that they are, to receive his Rain—to catch the Timeless Flow.

The Kingdom is coming. John told us, standing beside the smallish Jordan, seeing a Great River, speaking of that larger deluge that one day would inundate us—one bright day of darkness when the flood would finally wash away our earthen degradations.

  𝕚 𝕚 𝕚

Oh, yes, the Kingdom is coming, is *come*. It flows across our livid senses like a fragrant salve—that balm of Gilead which heals the sin-sick soul. *We are so sick with sin!* We, his people—weak with anemia, for the loss of his blood. Dyspeptic from the lies which we have swallowed, the hidden sins we cannot stomach, which taste sweet on the tongue and ulcerate our soul.

Our spirits die within us; the Spirit dies within us. We dress the Corpse, the hollow shell, the "whited sepulcher" we are with a smile and a word of prayer. We parade down our sacred aisles into our hallowed sanctuaries dressed in the emperor's clothes. You know—as I do, perhaps better than I—the crumbling pillars that support our church. Is there another Samson waiting in the narthex, ready to grope his way within?

The Kingdom is *coming*! Not by words, but by Power. All the words will be swept away, the fertile and chaff, and *Word* shall rise like great columns, to meet and hold his canopy of Peace—like massive arms, palms up and open beneath the converging Heavens.

The Kingdom rides a stronger Wind than we know. We have felt the force of gales which sweep the very pinnings of our lives from down beneath us. We stand too loosely now—too unconnected in this altered landscape to resist *it*. We are swept along by, swept into earth's contentions and contentiousness—but comes the Wind, scything through our bleak alternatives and glittering alterations to his Truth . . . .

The Winds of Heaven come! They gather at the corridors of his Eternity, rehearsing in the silent skies beyond us. Unleashed, they cannot be contained by our small stratosphere, or garnered by our plaintive protestations. We are undone—and Mercury, who rode the fabled winds of fantasy, would never countenance such violent splendor. Winds of this sort know only chaff. And chaff of this sort knows no weight in Heaven; a mighty column is a feather; the feather of a sparrow holds aloft his Temple.

Yes, It comes quickly now, its tempo paced to a new intensity. The saints both past and present wait with holy awe, sensing some new Presence, like a rain-scent on the laden air.

Stand still a moment. It comes to you, for you as well, this Great Dimension, like a promise kept, a dream fulfilled, a Home you knew . . . and lost . . . and ever yearned for.

The Kingdom is coming!